ABOUT THE AUTHOR

A former classical violinist at the Yehudi Menuhin School, Ben Renshaw now works as a therapist, trainer and writer, and is co-director of the Happiness Project. His work brings him into contact with leaders in the fields of business, health and education, as well as the wider general public, and he also appears regularly in the media. He lives in London.

D0235108

SUCCESSFUL BUT SOMETHING MISSING

Daring to enjoy life to the full

Ben Renshaw

VERMILION
LONDON

1 3 5 7 9 10 8 6 4 2

First published in 2000 by Rider,
an imprint of Ebury Press, Random House,
20 Vauxhall Bridge Road, London SW1V 2SA
www.randomhouse.co.uk
Reprinted in 2001 by Vermilion

Random House Australia (Pty) Limited
20 Alfred Street, Milsons Point, Sydney,
New South Wales 2061, Australia

Random House New Zealand Limited
18 Poland Road, Glenfield,
Auckland 10, New Zealand

Random House (Pty) Limited
Endulini, 5A Jubilee Road,
Parktown 2193, South Africa

The Random House Group Limited Reg. No. 954009

Back cover photograph © Martin Vallis

Papers used by Rider are natural, recyclable products
made from wood grown in sustainable forests.

Typeset by SX Composing DTP, Rayleigh, Essex
Printed and bound by Mackays of Chatham plc, Chatham, Kent

A CIP catalogue record for this book
is available from the British Library

ISBN 0-7126-7053-X

Dedicated to Veronica
for being there,
believing in me
and loving me.

Contents

Acknowledgements

True success is a team effort and it gives me great joy to be able to acknowledge everyone who has made this book possible. Starting with my family, thank you to my mother, Virginia, for willingly reading and rereading the manuscript, you are a true mum, and to her partner Alistair for always generating a laugh. Thank you to my father, Peter, for encouraging and inspiring me with your vision, and to his wife Milena, for her support. Thank you to my sister, Sophie, for your honesty and love, and her partner Kevin for his open heart. Thank you to my cousin Dave White, for your emotional courage and unfailing friendship, and his partner Debbie for being so real. Thank you to my cousin Eg White and his wife Polly, your friendship is a real gift. Thank you to Lucy White and her partner Juliet, for your unconditional love. Thank you to Veronica's parents Ron and Lucy Annan, I am blessed to have you as in laws. Thank you to Carl and Rose, Justine, Denise and Shane, Doug, Rick, Andre, Stu and Lindel, for being extended family.

Thank you to Robert Holden, your support and clarity is a priceless gift, and to his wife Miranda for holding the light. Thank you to The Happiness Project team: David Holden, for your strength and loyalty, Candy Constable, for your grace and willingness, Alison Atwell, for walking the same path, Sue Tait, for your zest for life. Thank you to all the helpers and participants at the Project for your commitment to happiness.

Thank you to Nick Williams, for your love and encouragement, and to your partner Helen Bee. Thank you to Louise Manson for your writing skill and expertise. Thank you to my past teachers, Sondra Ray, Diana Roberts, Bob and Mallie Mandel, Fred Lehrman, Peter and Meg Kane, Rhonda Levande:

your love and inspiration set me on the way. Thank you to Brian and Renee Elliott, for embodying true friendship. Thank you to Andy Thrasyvoulou for being the perfect buddy, and his wife Vasso. Thank you to Richard Field OBE, for always making the time. Thank you to Tom and Linda Carpenter, for being living examples of true success. Thank you to my chiropractor Stephen Hughes who kept putting me back together! Thank you to the many friends who have supported me along the way, Paul and Ondine Barrow, James Bennett, Heloise Bergman and my godson Zach, Didier, Kim and Annabella Boutet, Doug Boyes, John Briffa, Charlie Carne, Amanda Cohen, Steve Donahue, Yuval Goldenberg, Dorothy Krefta, Michael McQuilkin, Sara Novokovic, Eddie and Debbie Shapiro, Robin Woodsford, Simon Woodroffe, Andy and Pam Stevenson.

Thank you to my publishing team. Judith Kendra, for giving me the green light and showing me the way forward. Thank you to Barbara Bagnall for being so efficient. Thank you to Claire Bowles for your expert PR and enthusiasm. Thank you to Josephine Dawson for your marketing wisdom and support. Thank you to the sales reps for getting it on the road.

Foreword

by Robert Holden, author of *Happiness NOW!*

Do you remember the White Rabbit in Lewis Carroll's *Alice in Wonderland*? Alice is resting by a babbling brook on a perfect summer's afternoon. It is an idyllic moment. Nothing is missing. And, then, out of nowhere, the White Rabbit appears, 'Oh dear! Oh dear! I'm late, I'm late, for a very important date.' The peace is broken.

The White Rabbit runs and runs and runs, chasing after something. He is late, but he never makes up time. He hurries, but he never makes up ground. He strives, but he never arrives. All that effort gets him places but nowhere he really wants to be. So, here's the question: *do you ever catch yourself living your life like the White Rabbit?* If so, Ben Renshaw's book may be just the tonic you are looking for.

The story of the White Rabbit means a lot to both Ben and me. As co-directors of The Happiness Project we teach many of our courses at Oxford University where Lewis Carroll spent much of his time. Indeed, from our room, we can see an old seventeenth-century stone passageway which is said to be the inspiration for the White Rabbit's many entrances and exits.

The White Rabbit is a metaphor for the part of your mind – the ego – which believes Everything Good is Outside. In other words, the ego is a belief that success, inspiration, peace, love, creativity, wisdom, happiness, God and all things great are *somewhere else* other than inside you! This single erroneous belief creates an illusion of personal lack. We become beggars on a beach of gold. Our ego is our greatest block to success.

In this book, Ben Renshaw challenges you to rethink success and to take a look again at who you really are. What if nothing is missing? What if you already have everything it takes to be happy, to be successful? What if, success is not a chase, but a state of mind? Success is a journey, Ben says.

Ben Renshaw is my friend and my inspiration. His work in education, health care and business is fast becoming legendary. He is a truly gifted coach, consultant, healer, broadcaster and speaker. He lives his message in an honest, humble and human way. He's one of us, and he's telling us we all have what it takes to enjoy life to the full.

I hope you enjoy this book. Read it slowly. Let it inspire you. It has many gifts to give you.

Introduction

REDEFINING SUCCESS

What would you like to hear first, the good news or the better news? Well, the good news is that, if you feel something is missing in your life, it isn't. And the better news is that you have simply been looking in the wrong place!

From an early age my life was spent at the Yehudi Menuhin School as a violinist. I would rise each morning to start practising before breakfast. I invested hour after hour, day after day developing my technique and musical expression as I aspired to be a great musician. You couldn't fault me for effort or hard work, I paid my dues. When it came to a concert the adrenalin flowed as I strove to achieve the perfect performance. On the final flourish I would receive the applause and be on a high. Once the euphoria wore off though, I would be left feeling confused and angst-ridden.

I came to realise that I had worked hard to be successful without having worked out what success really was. I believed that if I achieved enough, accumulated enough and received enough recognition then I would be successful. Unfortunately, enough was never enough, and like James Bond I concluded that even 'The world is not enough'! Having pursued that route for many years without reaching a finishing line it came as something of a shock for me to recognise that true success is not 'out there' in the world but it is to be found within us.

If you have placed your best bet for success on your achievements, possessions, work or relationships, you have been seeing the source of what you want as outside yourself. It is comparable to climbing a ladder of success, only to find that you have been leaning it against the wrong wall! Now is the time to shift your awareness. In order to be successful and truly happy it is essential that you turn your focus inward and recognise that these states already exist within you. It is a journey without distance. Your job is to strip away the illusions that have cloaked these gifts. Picture the existence of the sun. Just because you don't always see it does not mean that it isn't always there, always shining and always radiant.

Before reading on, take a look at the following statement and register what you see:

SUCCESSISNOWHERE

How did you read this statement, 'success is nowhere', or 'success is now here'? The key to transforming your relationship to success has something to do with the events in your life and everything to do with how you see them. In other words, everything in the world can encourage you to be successful, for example having a loving family, a beautiful home, a fast car, financial security, fulfilling work and exotic holidays, but nothing can make you successful. This is because true success is a state of mind, not an achievement. I have met and worked with millionaires and managing directors who are still searching for their first meaningful success. I have also met and worked with people who have achieved very little outward success, but who live their life as if they were blessed with all the riches in the world.

The major difference between these two types of people is in how they perceive their life. The person who is striving for success but never arriving sees the world through lenses of doom and gloom predominantly, spotting the problems in everything and predicting the worst. They see their glass as half empty. The person who experiences success on a daily basis sees the world through lenses of opportunity: they catch themselves and others doing things right and they let good things happen. They see their glass as half full. So who is right, the optimist or the pessimist? The truth is that they both are. The law of perception is to be careful what you look for because you will find it. If you look for success, success will find you. Or if you look for another reason to prevent you from recognising success, you will find that also.

This book will show you how to reorientate your attitude in a way that will make fulfilment possible on all levels. The process of changing your outlook towards success takes a small amount of 'how to' and a large amount of 'want to' – your willingness is the key. If you notice yourself feeling slightly cynical about new ideas and possibilities, I would like you to reflect on whether you believe that you were born a cynic. My personal research is to find a cynical baby and I have yet to discover one! I believe that our essential nature is one of happiness, love and joy, but these can get knocked out of us over the years. The journey of being successful and truly happy is to discover and recover our natural state of hope, optimism and creativity.

Life Is On Our Side

Sometimes it is possible to see our life as a fight against the world in which we are engaged in a heavyweight bout that is going the full fifteen rounds. If you resonate with this image you need to pivot 180 degrees in your thinking and embrace the idea that life is on your side.

The truth is that the world wants you to succeed and to be happy. The responsibility lies with you to open yourself to this possibility. If you believe that life is against you, you become defensive and closed, and block opportunities from occurring. Even if success is staring you in the face you might fail to see it because your attention is elsewhere. You may tend to feel cut off from a natural flow in life and experience it as a series of struggles. Your work may seem like a punishment, your relationships may appear to be a source of conflict, and good health may seem to elude you.

This can occur because you have set yourself up, within your own mind, in opposition to natural principles that bring you what you want. You do not have to know how they work at this stage, any more than you need to know how a computer, electricity or gravity really works. You can still use them and enjoy the benefits. The Greek philosopher Heraclitus wrote: 'There is only one wisdom: to recognise the intelligence that steers all things.' It is this intelligence that causes our bodies to function, birds to fly and flowers to grow, and which brings dreams and desires to fruition. It has infinite organising power, so the more tuned into it you are, the more access you have to unlimited creativity. By consciously connecting with this intelligence your relationships, work and life will be transformed.

Change Your Mind, Change Your Life

> The greatest discovery of my generation is that a human being can alter his life by altering his attitude. *William James*, psychologist and philosopher

So the starting point in creating a new experience in life is to change the way that we see things. In order to change our experience of success we need to redefine our current thinking about it. We have received many different messages from our past conditioning, some of which are useful whilst others prevent us from feeling successful. As you read the following table, see which ideas you resonate with and consider the influence they have had upon you.

TABLE 1

Old paradigm about success	Influence
Success is an 'outer' state.	We search continuously for success outside ourselves.
Success is an achievement.	Our self-esteem and identity become linked to what we accomplish.
Success is about 'doing' and 'having'.	We keep busy and wanting more

Success is linked to wealth and status.	We measure people by their bank balance and position.
Success is by judged by comparison with others; it is relative.	We assess ourselves according to how we perceive others.
The person who gets the most wins.	This creates competition and win/lose thinking.
Success is hard to get.	We struggle, strive and push.
Success is never enough.	It creates no satisfaction, no enjoyment and no peace.

As you will discover during the course of this book, awareness is the starting point for change. To become aware of this old conditioning and its influence enables you to make new choices about what you want to focus on. Table 2 presents a new model of thinking, which enables you to be successful and truly happy:

TABLE 2

New paradigm for success	Influence
Success is an 'inner' state.	We stop searching for success outside ourselves.
Success is a state of mind.	Our self-esteem and identity are linked to our attitude, not to our achievements.

Success is being true to ourselves.	Focus on 'being' rather than on proving ourselves.
Success is not limited to the accumulation of material possessions.	We are motivated by giving and opening ourselves to others.
Success is not a competition.	This creates co-operation, win/win thinking and synergy.
Success is about giving our heart and receiving in abundance.	We focus on giving rather than getting.
Success can be graceful and joyous.	It encourages ease, relaxation and non-attachment.
Success is enough.	It creates fulfilment, enjoyment and peace.

Getting the Balance Right

In the old paradigm the primary criterion for success is linked to 'doing' and 'having'. We believed that if we did enough and had enough, we would be happy. The new paradigm emphasises the importance of 'being', which includes qualities such as love, truth, simplicity, integrity, authenticity, giving and compassion. The act of balancing 'doing' with 'being' enables us to experience true success in all areas of life, including family, work, play and spirituality.

A useful way to monitor this balance is to ask yourself the following types of question: 'Would I trade money for love?' 'Would I trade ambition for integrity?' 'Would I trade recognition for authenticity?' Your rational mind would probably answer 'no'; it would acknowledge the importance of the qualities of 'being', yet in the busyness of your life it is easy to forget what is truly important. We need constant reminders to keep ourselves on track and to resist putting 'being' on the back burner as we get on with our busy and demanding lives.

Take a Quantum Leap!

We live in a world of constant uncertainty. In fact, the only guarantee today is change. In order to rise to this challenge we need to draw on personal reservoirs of strength and self-belief that enable us to move forward with confidence. It can take a leap of faith to recognise that you do have a choice about how to get what you want in life. Either you can struggle, strive and push forward, or you can choose the path of least resistance, which requires you to be willing to go out on a limb and trust the process of life.

To trust in the power that created you, whether you call it God as you understand God, love, essence or spirit, allows you to let go of the fears, doubts and insecurities that prevent you from enjoying true happiness and success. I believe that by turning your attention back to the miracle of your own creation you form the building blocks for the development of trust. Through reflecting upon the synchronicity of a specific sperm and egg fusing to give you life, you become aware of another force at play here.

More and more people are now interested in the spiritual dimension of life. Science and technology have enabled us to make vast improvements in our standard of living but they don't entirely fill the void that many of us experience. This gap is where we have become disconnected from our spiritual selves. By strengthening our awareness of spirit we are also strengthened by it.

Some of the practical ways to raise our awareness of spirit in daily life include:

◆ Spending time in nature. Even if you are living in a city you have the opportunity to walk in a park, look at trees, marvel at flowers, gaze at grass and watch the sky, sun, moon and stars. As you do so, notice the intelligence within every living thing. Reflect on the miracle of the creation of nature.

◆ Taking time to be silent, to just *be*. You might like to learn to meditate. If you already do so then you are aware of the power of silence, stillness and reflection. Being silent quietens your mind and enables you to put your focus on what is truly important in your life.

◆ Practising mindfulness. Mindfulness is concerned with simply being aware of and living in this present moment. We spend so much of our time either 'stuck' in the past or worrying about the future that we are rarely fully present in the here and now. The practice of mindfulness involves noticing thoughts, feelings and events in your life, while letting go of your attachment to the outcome. Since your full creative power lies in the present moment, the more you give to now the more you receive from now.

◆ Developing your creativity. We all have creative potential; this is not limited to the arts. Seeing yourself as a creative being aligns you with the creative energy of spirit.

Success Starts at Home

So many of our challenges stem from a basic unhappiness with our own selves. Until you learn to like yourself, nothing will essentially change. Unhappiness can also come from a lack of understanding of how our emotional structure works and how we can learn to work *with* – rather than just react *to* our feelings. Our relationships with others reflect our feelings about ourselves; through learning how to improve communication and resolve difficulties in a loving, rather than confrontational way, we can enjoy greater intimacy. Finally, work forms a very large part of our lives: what we do is hugely important to us all. If work feels like a struggle or a battlefield, there are things you can do to turn it into a deeply fulfilling part of your life. By approaching yourself, your feelings, your relationship and your work from *inside* rather than *outside*, you can find the missing piece of your own jigsaw.

Successful But Something Missing offers practical exercises and ideas to remove the blocks to being successful and truly happy, which is our natural inheritance. By using the tools in this book I have discovered that ultimately success is a journey, not a destination. I encourage you to go within and enjoy the adventure of a lifetime!

1

Simply You!

Your goal is to find out who you are. *A Course in Miracles*

The most important relationship you have in life is with yourself. The world is a mirror that reflects back to you your own state of mind. For most of your life you may have been facing the wrong way, looking outside yourself for success and happiness. If so, you now have the opportunity to turn around, direct your attention inwards and discover that what you have been seeking has been within you all along.

When I began the journey of self-awareness, I was both apprehensive and optimistic about what I might find. I wanted to know the truth, yet at the same time I experienced resistance to it. In the back of my mind was a fear that there was some dark hidden secret about myself, which if revealed would be insurmountable. Thankfully this fear has never materialised. What I have witnessed is that as you peel away the layers of conditioning you learn that the truth about yourself is a wonderful surprise. The following prayer, from *Seasons of Your Heart* by Macrina Wiederkehr, is a helpful reminder to keep an open mind about who you really are: 'O God, help me to believe the truth about myself, no matter how beautiful it is. Amen.'

When you make this shift in focus you arrive at an understanding of the Buddhist wisdom, *wherever you go, there you are.* You can spend many years of your life running away only to find that you arrive back at where you started: with yourself. In today's world there are many temptations that can prevent you from turning your attention inward. Work is the most socially acceptable way of keeping yourself distracted from looking closely at who you are. Other activities that can keep you preoccupied include shopping, sport, travel, DIY, addictive substances such as alcohol, drugs and nicotine, television and general busyness.

The quality of your relationship with yourself influences the quality of your relationship with everything. Being at peace with yourself allows you to be at peace with the world. Feeling successful within yourself allows you to enjoy your success in the world. Being happy with yourself allows you to be happy in the world. The key to determining the quality of your relationship with yourself is governed by two different states of mind: the ego mind and the Higher Self. What you believe about yourself is determined by which state of mind you are in. In *The Tibetan Book of Living and Dying*, Sogyal Rinpoche gives an insightful account of this dynamic: 'Two people have been living in you all of your life. One is the ego, garrulous, demanding, hysterical, calculating; the other is the hidden spiritual being, whose still voice of wisdom you have only rarely heard or attended to.'

These two states of mind are given many different names. The ego is known as the false self, the lower self, the unreal self, the persona, the judge, the chatterbox and the conditioned self. The higher mind is known as the Higher Self, the true self, the real self, the creative self, the unconditioned self, the whole self and spirit. It is not important which label you use. The importance lies in becoming aware of them, so that you can make the leap from living in the ego to living in spirit. We will now look at this awareness in greater depth since it is the foundation of our success.

THE EGO

The ego is an extraordinary concept because it has such a powerful influence over our lives, yet no one has ever found or seen the ego. This is because it is no more than an idea based on the belief that there is something missing. When you project the ego on to yourself, you believe that there is something missing within you. This causes you to look outside yourself for success and happiness. The ego sees itself as separate from everything and everyone. As a result you see yourself as an isolated being cut off from the world around you. This is a myth, since it is impossible for you to be separate from the source. The study of quantum physics shows that we are all connected on a molecular level. The idea of separation is an illusion.

When you are trapped in the ego, you fear lack and scarcity.

When you see life through the lens of the ego all that you see is fear, fear and more fear! Since fear clouds your perception, you no longer see things as they really are. This explains why, when you get what you want in your life, but are caught in the ego, all that you see are fearful consequences. You can achieve success and fear failure. You can have enough money and fear lack. You can receive love and fear rejection. Robert Holden calls this the 'lack attack'.

The function of the ego is to keep you lost and hidden from your true self. It is the cloud in the sky that blocks the sun. When you are caught in the ego it is like being lost in a forest and not being able to find your way out. The ego's motto is 'Seek, but do not find'. So we keep striving for success (but never arriving) and we want more (but more is never enough). The ego keeps us away from peace of mind and fulfilment, and is at the root of who most of us believe we are.

There are four primary ways in which the ego impacts on the relationship we have with ourselves.

Self-judgement

When you judge yourself, you are denying the truth about yourself and causing yourself unnecessary suffering. This is a learned behaviour that can become habitual, and it is detrimental to your wellbeing. It is the voice within you that nags you, disapproves of you and is hard on you.

Let's look at how self-judgement operates. If you walk into a room filled with people and feel small and insignificant this is the voice of self-judgement telling you that you do not belong, you have nothing of importance to say and no one is interested in you.

You go for a job interview and tell yourself that you do not have the ability, personality and experience for the position before you've even tried. You meet someone you are attracted to and see yourself as unattractive and not clever enough; you believe that there is no chance that they will be interested in you. As long as you continue to judge yourself you will not see who you really are.

I worked with a client called Ray who suffered from chronic self-judgement. He called it the 'chatterbox' because it never seemed to leave him alone. The only time that he got respite was when he was asleep, but as soon as he woke up it started up again. A common experience for Ray was as follows: he would wake up and immediately feel anxious, as if he had done something wrong, or feel that he wouldn't be able to cope that day. It did not seem to matter what Ray accomplished during a day: he would always feel that he should be doing better. He judged his appearance, job position, relationships and lifestyle as being not good enough, so he never allowed himself to enjoy his life fully. He felt as if he was living in hell, whatever external changes he made in his life.

Recognising your self-judgement is the first step in freeing and releasing yourself from it. Each time you catch yourself in judgement remind yourself that it is a negative pattern that moves you away from your true self. Appreciate and value yourself *now*, rather than when you have corrected all your perceived faults: this way you heal the judgement that has caused you to forget who you really are.

Self-attack

Rebecca came to me suffering from bouts of depression and low self-esteem. As we discussed her experience she became aware of how she attacked herself. She would deprive herself of what she wanted because she didn't think that she deserved it. She would force herself to work longer hours to punish herself for feeling unworthy. Rebecca was a 'people pleaser', putting aside her own interests and concerns in order to do what others wanted. At first she found it painful to admit this, but by understanding that such behaviour is learned and can be resolved, it became more painful to hold on to it than to create new habits.

Begin to notice if you attack yourself in either covert or overt ways. Recognising this can activate feelings of shame and embarrassment, which cause you to try and hide or cover up your behaviour. This is very common and is the ego's way of preventing you from getting appropriate support. Simply sharing your feelings and behaviour with a therapist or loving friend, or in a support group can transform the way that you treat yourself.

Self-doubt

The ego thrives on doubt. It questions your intuition, your talent, your creativity and your happiness to such an extent that you can lose your self-belief. Self-doubt causes you to withdraw from situations that encourage you to shine.

I observed self-doubt in a client called Paul. He would become shy, reserved and withdrawn. He would find it difficult to communicate and checked himself before he spoke and apologised after speaking. He could not develop rewarding relationships since he was not able to establish a close rapport with the people around him. Doubt is a traitor because it imposes unnecessary limitations on our lives. Opening your mind to the endless opportunities and possibilities in life lays your doubts to rest.

Self-sabotage

Sometimes, just as we are about to get what we want, or we have finally achieved what we want, we blow it. Without being conscious of it, we've set limits, like a thermostat, so that when things get *too good* the thermostat kicks in to cool us down and bring us back to what is familiar. Behind all sabotage is either guilt or fear of loss. The guilt is based on the erroneous belief that we don't deserve something, and the fear is that if we do have it we will lose something. Both have their roots in feelings of low self-worth, so the way through is to increase our self-esteem.

There are many examples in today's culture of how we

sabotage our happiness and success. In particular those people who achieve outer success very quickly are prone to sabotage it because it does not match their self-concept. People in pop music, the film industry and the sporting world who earn fame and fortune at a young age are susceptible because the change in reality can be too fast for them to integrate.

In order to end self-sabotage you must be willing to change your mind about yourself and see that you are worthy of happiness and success.

Core Negative Beliefs

The ego is an unreasonable and irrational state of mind. It is an uncomfortable experience to be caught in the ego and yet it is very common since from an early age we have been conditioned to believe that there is something missing within us. Unless our parents were enlightened masters we probably received messages such as 'you're not good enough', 'you're imperfect', 'you have to shape up' and 'you're wrong'. This was probably compounded at school by teachers implying that we're stupid, insignificant, a nuisance and bad. No blame of parents or teachers is intended here; I am aware of the challenge of these roles and also by the fact that parents and teachers are products of their own conditioning. But these types of message have been passed down for generations, resulting in the majority of us suffering from wrong thinking about ourselves. The media and consumer society we live in certainly hasn't helped by pumping out images that feed our insecurities, doubts and cravings for more.

As a result of this conditioning I have observed some common core negative beliefs that we hold about ourselves, which act as self-fulfilling prophecies in the world of the ego. It is valuable to become aware of these so that we can make new choices to connect with the truth about ourselves. We create entire stories based on these beliefs and they become the way we see ourselves. As we identify these stories it is important to remember that they are myths – illusions that we have made up – and the reason that they feel real is because we have believed them to be true. The most common phrases with which people deceive themselves are:

(1) 'I'm not good enough'; (2) 'There's something wrong with me'; (3) 'I'm unworthy'; (4) 'I'm a failure'. They may sound fairly similar, and are, but as we look closely at each, watch to see if you identify with one in particular.

'I'm not good enough'

This is definitely the number one hit on the ego parade. 'I'm not good enough' is the root cause of more feelings of failure, rejection, despondency and anxiety then any other thought. The words to the 'I'm not good enough' song are as follows:

◆ Everything I do is not good enough, my work is not creative enough and my achievements aren't high enough.
◆ Everything I say isn't good enough, my conversation is limited and my listening ability is lacking.
◆ Everything I have isn't good enough, I haven't got enough time, I haven't got enough money, my home isn't large enough, my wardrobe isn't stylish enough and my car is not fast enough.
◆ Physically, I am not attractive enough: my thighs are too big, my legs are too small, my hair is too curly, my skin is too wrinkly and my eyes are too dark.
◆ Mentally, I am not clever enough, intelligent enough and smart enough.
◆ Emotionally, I am not peaceful enough, happy enough, joyful enough and funny enough.
◆ Spiritually, I haven't meditated enough, prayed enough, chanted enough and purified myself enough.

The 'I'm not good enough' story consists of one judgement after another. It is exhausting, demoralising, frustrating and untrue. The ego thrives on this belief because it keeps you searching outside of yourself for answers.

Nothing is ever enough, as long as you continue to believe that you are not good enough.

Steve was a client who had experienced a painful separation from a long-term relationship several months before and was feeling depressed, listless and tense. His core negative belief was that he was not good enough, and as a result he felt a failure, unattractive and that his life was slipping away. When Steve tried to talk about the relationship he quickly fell into self-judgement, blaming himself for how it broke down. He compared himself to other men and felt that he was inferior because he believed that he was unattractive, unintelligent and boring to be with.

All judgements are learned.

When we looked at Steve's history it transpired that these were the messages he had received from his parents. No matter how hard he tried to please them he could never live up to their expectations. He felt a tremendous sense of pressure to achieve and lead a successful life. Yet whenever he did anything of note, they compared him to his sister, who was a grade A student and who could do no wrong. Steve perceived himself as not good enough and everything about his life as not good enough. His coping mechanism became to judge himself even more. Subconsciously he believed that if he judged himself enough then it would make him a good enough person and he wouldn't suffer any more rejection.

We looked at Steve's resistance to releasing the judgement. His major barrier was his belief that he didn't deserve to let it go. He felt guilty about being such a failure (in his mind) and wanted to punish himself. The judgement was his way of doing this. We discovered that he was waiting for the ultimate Judgment Day when he was to stand in front of God and be assessed. He was so afraid of being damned that he felt if he kept judging himself now, then God would let him off and he would be saved. He perceived God as a disapproving old man living up in the sky who was watching his every move. He was convinced that God saw him as a failure too.

Steve found talking about his experience very helpful. He had kept it private because he felt so ashamed of his thoughts and feelings. He had judged them as another sign of his weakness and didn't want them to be revealed. To be able to disclose them in the presence of another person and to experience being accepted was a profound moment for him. It helped him to entertain the possibility that maybe he *was* good enough after all and that these judgements were fabrications of his imagination.

Steve learned that the major key to unlocking this pattern was to recognise that the judgement was in the ego mind and that he was projecting it on to his parents, God and the world in the hope of his salvation. He admitted that by ending the judgement he could see the truth about himself – that he is good enough just the way he is.

'There's something wrong with me'

Some days it can feel as if you are walking around with an invisible sign scrawled across your forehead saying, 'Please tell me what's wrong with me.' Picture two doors, one with a sign saying 'What's wrong with me?' and the second with a sign saying 'What's right with me?' Which door would you open first? The temptation is to go through the first door because we believe that if we can find out what is wrong with us, then we will know how to 'fix' ourselves. The trouble is that since the belief 'There's something wrong with me' is a mistake, we continue to go around in circles. By letting it go we can experience who we really are.

Symptoms of this storyline include the following:

- You perceive any mishap in your life as evidence that there's something wrong with you.
- You translate any form of rejection into proof that there's something wrong with you.
- You consistently feel wrong: in your work, relationships, home and life.
- You worry about getting ill.
- You reject praise and compliments because they don't fit your picture of yourself.
- You catch yourself doing things wrong, but overlook it when you are doing things right.
- You enjoy arguing 'right and wrong' issues.
- You overcompensate by trying to be right and defending yourself if you are in the wrong.

I worked with a client, Billy, whose entire life had been dominated by this erroneous belief. While he was growing up he felt as if everyone who noticed him commented on what was wrong with him, which made him extremely self-conscious. He believed that he always had the wrong haircut, wore the wrong clothes, said the wrong things, had the wrong friends and got his work wrong at school. As an adult he prevented himself from doing what he really wanted to do because he believed that it was the wrong thing. Whenever he entered a relationship he would sabotage it by believing that there was something wrong with it. He had even tried living in different countries – but each one appeared to be the wrong one.

By being able to identify the belief and the effects of the belief so clearly, Billy could accept that the real cause of his dilemma was the wrong thinking he held about himself. His willingness to change his mind and see himself differently was the turning point for him to transform his life.

'I'm unworthy'

Groucho Marx personified this belief when he declared that he would not join any club that would have him as a member! When you carry this belief you either see yourself as being unworthy or you project it on to others and perceive them as unworthy. This belief gives rise to the majority of low self-esteem and lack of confidence that people experience.

The common effects of the 'I'm unworthy' story include the following:

◆ You believe that you are unworthy and don't deserve to get what you want in life.
◆ You punish yourself if you do receive something that doesn't fit your picture of how you see yourself.
◆ You put yourself down, and withdraw when asked your opinion.
◆ You sabotage your success and happiness.
◆ You feel each project you complete is worthless.
◆ You constantly seek others' approval because you cannot approve of yourself.

- You are a 'people pleaser' because you hope that you will gain some love.
- You over-compensate by trying to prove you are the best.

'I'm a failure'

There are two primary ways in which this belief affects our lives. Either we act it out and 'fail' in our lives, or we overcompensate and achieve outer success but always have a feeling of failure. I had a client, Edward, who displayed the signs of success mixed with a belief of failure. By his mid-thirties he had achieved everything that he wanted in his life. He was managing director of his own successful company, he had a high standard of living and he was financially independent. Yet he felt an utter failure and was unable to enjoy the benefits of his work since his perception of himself was so low. Edward realised that he had to change this belief that he was a failure. By being willing to change his mind about himself, Edward started to enjoy the success that he had created.

Common symptoms of this belief include the following:

- You underachieve in your life to prove that you are a failure.
- You turn down opportunities when they are presented to you because you think you can't handle them.
- You have low self-esteem and confidence.
- You fail to trust your own instincts because you think they will let you down.
- You do not believe that you can have a lasting loving relationship. You fear that all your relationships will end in failure.
- You compare yourself to your colleagues and friends and see yourself as lesser.

As well as these four negative beliefs there are other variations: beliefs such as 'I'm bad', 'I'm guilty', 'I'm strange and different' and 'I'm unlovable' can surface as people weed out their false perceptions of self.

Exercise: To locate your core negative belief, answer the following questions by writing down the first response that comes into your mind.

A negative belief I have about myself is . . .
The negative belief I am afraid others will have about me is . . .
The negative belief I resist applying to myself is . . .
My most negative belief about myself is . . .

Circle the one that has the most meaning for you. This is your core negative belief. Having discovered what it is, your commitment now lies in choosing to change your mind about yourself. *A Course in Miracles* makes this point very clear: 'Your mission is very simple. You are asked to live so as to demonstrate that you are not an ego.'

Moving from the ego to the Higher Self

A helpful technique to change your mind about yourself is **affirmations**. Affirmations are positive statements that you immerse in your consciousness by the use of repetition. There are two main reasons for working with affirmations. Firstly, they encourage you to focus on the truth about yourself, and, secondly, they help you to let go of any resistance you may have to changing your mind about yourself.

Some examples of affirmations to use in relation to the four core negative beliefs are:

◆ I am good enough as I am.
◆ I am right exactly as I am.
◆ I am worthy.
◆ I am a success.

When you first start working with these types of thoughts you will probably experience some cynicism and disbelief. This is perfectly natural since you have held a different image of yourself for so many years. You need to give yourself time to allow these new thoughts to sink in. The way to create an affirmation is to decide on the belief that you want to affirm and to put it in the present tense, making sure that it is personal and positive. A good way to work with affirmations is to write them out. Draw a line down the middle of a page; on the left-hand side write the affirmation and on the right-hand side write down the first response you have to the affirmation, as shown in Table 3.

TABLE 3

Affirmation	Response
I am good enough.	But I don't feel it.
I am good enough.	But I haven't achieved enough.
I am good enough.	I don't believe it!
I am good enough.	Sometimes.
I am good enough.	'Enough' is not good enough.
I am good enough.	Maybe.
I am good enough.	I'm willing to believe it.
I am good enough.	Now I can relax!

Picture affirmations as seeds that you are planting in the garden of your mind. The response column is the tending that you need to do in order to allow the seeds to germinate, grow and eventually flower. The affirmation helps you to experience who you really are since it encourages you to accept the truth about yourself. I recommend that you write an affirmation ten times a day for one week. This gives it enough time to sink into your subconscious mind.

An important aspect of using affirmations is that they connect you with the principle that you are a creative being and you are fully responsible for the choices you make. An affirmation is a creative choice to see the truth about yourself. This choice is your source of power and freedom and is clearly illustrated in Dr Victor Frankl's book, *Man's Search for Meaning*. Frankl was a psychiatrist and a Jew who survived the horrors of the Nazi death camps. In his book, a moving account of his experiences, he wrote:

In the concentration camp every circumstance conspires to make the prisoner lose his hold. All the familiar goals in life are snatched away. What alone remains is the last of the human freedoms – the ability to choose one's attitude in a given set of circumstances, to choose one's own way.

The choice to undo your conditioned thinking about yourself enables you to fulfil your human potential and embrace who you really are.

The Choice to Let Go

A choice that complements your willingness to see yourself differently is the choice to forgive yourself for identifying so closely with the ego. Forgiveness is the mental technique by which you undo your wrong thinking. Believing that you are an ego and that you are your negative beliefs is a form of wrong thinking. Forgiving yourself for having had this perception sets you free and allows you to accept the idea that you are whole and perfect as you are, thus connecting you with your Higher Self. The willingness to forgive yourself is the willingness to see the truth about yourself. As you let go of self-judgement you let go of the need to condemn yourself, put yourself down and be hard on yourself. All these are forms of self-attack and bring you conflict and pain. Forgiveness is the solvent that melts this self-attack and restores your sense of sanity.

Through the practice of forgiveness you witness the ego and

its insane thinking. The power of noticing and observing the ego helps you to alter your perception of it. Since you are now observing it at work you are detaching yourself from its effects. You no longer see yourself as the ego: being able to witness it allows you to accept it. Acceptance is a vital ingredient in letting it go because if you resist the ego, it will persist. Accept it and you liberate yourself from the belief that it is real. Remember that the ego is just an idea that something is missing.

The final stage of transforming the ego identity is to extend love to it by deciding to treat it with kindness. This completely catches it off guard, surprising and disarming it. Extending love to the ego is an act of defencelessness, and is where your true safety lies. The ego cannot attack you when you are extending love to it. Your negative beliefs cannot harm you when you are extending love to them. The intention to make love more important than anything else connects you with your Higher Self.

THE HIGHER SELF

The Higher Self is who you really are. It is the experience of your whole, unconditioned self, the part of you that has been untouched by the world and lives in total harmony. As Aldous Huxley, the English author, beautifully expressed it, 'We do our best to disprove the fact, but a fact it remains; man is as divine as nature, as infinite as the void.'

The Higher Self is the sun behind the clouds and it is available to us 24 hours a day. There is no fear or belief in lack, scarcity and limitation in the world of the Higher Self since it is joined with spirit, which is infinite. Artists often refer to the experience of being connected with the Higher Self as being in the 'flow'. It is as if once we are released from our limited perceptions of self, the flow moves in. The composer Johannes Brahms captured this state when he said, 'Straight away the ideas flow in upon me, directly from God.' We do not have to be working artists in order to have this experience of flow and connection to the Higher Self. There are many opportunities in life which encourage us to connect with it. These include:

Being in nature. To spend time in nature is the simplest way to reconnect with your essential self. Feeling the earth under your feet, listening to the birds singing, observing the perfection of flowers and witnessing the longevity of trees all remind you of what is real and true.

Meditation. Being silent and still allows you to become aware of the presence of peace, which is the essence of the Higher Self.

Prayer. To pray is a method of affirming your intention by communing directly with God (as you understand God). I have found it the most effective way of reaching for peace when I am experiencing a troubled mind.

Listening. Truly listening to somebody else by putting yourself in their shoes opens your heart and takes you away from indulging in the ego.

Love-making. Sexual union and intimacy is a powerful way to transcend the ego and connect with the life force, also known as 'chi', 'prana' and 'kundalini'.

Serving mankind. Service is the highest form of giving. As you give selflessly you come to know your true self.

Living In the Higher Self

When you live in the Higher Self you experience a radical shift in your perception of yourself. You come to let go of your negative beliefs and you accept your perfection, creativity, inspiration and wisdom as true reflections of yourself. Living in your Higher Self gives you the freedom to enjoy true success because in the world of the Higher Self you are already successful. There is nothing that you have to do in order to prove your worth, there is nothing that you have to achieve in order to be a success and there is nothing that you have to get in order to be happy. Your worth, your success and your happiness all lie within the realms of your Higher Self. It is the treasure trove of all your dreams and wishes.

Making Peace with Yourself

People often ask, how do I know when I am living in the Higher Self? The simplest way to check is this: if you are experiencing peace of mind, it is a reflection of the Higher Self. If you are in conflict, it is the ego at work. The inspirational teacher Dr Wayne Dyer defined enlightenment as 'To be immersed in and surrounded by peace'. Through making peace with yourself you come to experience your true success.

To be at peace with yourself means that you have relinquished the four main effects of the ego: self-judgement, attack, doubt and sabotage. The extent to which you are affected by of one of these patterns is the extent to which you will be in conflict with yourself. Being at peace is being commited to seeing the truth about yourself no matter what is going on in your life at the time. This is particularly challenging when you don't seem to be getting what you want in your life.

Making peace with yourself means taking responsibility for your life.

You might shy away from taking responsibility for your life because you feel afraid of being held accountable. There is another way of looking at the word responsibility – 'response-ability' – the ability to choose your response. When you are experiencing self-conflict, taking responsibility means that you can choose a response in order to make peace with yourself. It is often tempting to have a 'victim mentality': you are tempted either to blame yourself, or to blame circumstances or other people for your inner conflict.

There are situations in which you genuinely experience being a victim: for example, if you have suffered physical, mental or emotional abuse, or an addiction that is beyond your control. But even then you have a choice about how you respond to the abuse or addiction.

Nicky came to see me at a time when there was good reason for her to have a victim mentality. She had recently survived an operation for cancer and was going through a painful divorce. When we looked at how to resolve the different areas of conflict she saw that to take responsibility and make peace with herself was the key. She felt guilty for the breakdown of the marriage, even though it had got to the stage where she feared for her physical safety. Her mother and local vicar were blaming her for the divorce and she felt alone and isolated since her children were taking the side of their father. To make peace with herself she accepted her own share of responsibility for each relationship and chose to see the lesson in each one. We labelled each relationship so that she could see the dynamic being acted out. Mother was the 'disapproving teacher', since she criticised everything Nicky did. Her vicar was the 'punishing head', since he blamed her for the choices she made, and her ex-husband was described as the 'victim child', since he was acting childishly and blaming her for the separation.

By accepting her own share of responsibility Nicky found a way to move forward. She could stop blaming herself and let go of the conflict she was carrying within. As she was able to make peace with herself she made peace with the other areas in her life. Making a different choice was a big commitment for her. She recognised that staying in a victim mentality would keep her repeating the same patterns, and her desire to experience peace kept her focused and on track.

Making peace with yourself is a life-changing decision. *A Course in Miracles* says, 'I want the peace of God. To say these words is nothing. But to mean these words is everything.' This level of commitment enables you to make peace with yourself. Each time you are tempted to judge or blame yourself in any shape or form, make the decision that peace is more important than anything else.

> **Exercise**: Ask yourself, 'What do I need to let go of in order to make peace with myself?'

Forgiving Yourself

Forgiveness is the method by which you stop seeing yourself as an ego and start seeing your wholeness and perfection. Forgiveness reconnects you to peace because it enables you to let go of the unloving thoughts you have about yourself. When you catch yourself judging yourself, forgive yourself. When you catch yourself attacking yourself, forgive yourself. When you catch yourself doubting yourself, forgive yourself and when you catch yourself sabotaging yourself, forgive yourself. Forgiveness is a full-time job and sometimes you might find it difficult. Resistance can surface which blocks you from letting go of the judgement you are holding on to. Remember to forgive yourself if you do experience resistance because what you resist, persists.

Forgiveness undoes judgement

Forgiveness is a process of selective remembering, a conscious decision to remember only loving thoughts about yourself and to let go of any fearful ones. I once worked with a client called John who suffered from large amounts of self-judgement and con-demnation. When he came to see me he had already taken the first step in letting go of the judgement by taking responsibility for it and recognising that it was in his power to relinquish it. This is vitally important, otherwise you see yourself as a helpless victim, which disempowers you. The next step for John was to choose to forgive himself. For two weeks I asked him to write down ten judgements that he was willing to forgive himself for each day. His list included statements such as:

◆ I forgive myself for judging myself.
◆ I forgive myself for thinking that I'm not good enough.
◆ I forgive myself for believing that everything is my fault.
◆ I forgive myself for feeling a failure.
◆ I forgive myself for being so hard on myself.

John did resist the idea of forgiveness at first. He felt that it was a cop-out and that he really should be punished for his perceived shortcomings. He didn't believe the forgiveness when he wrote it down and felt that he was just going through the motions. By the second week he noticed that the resistance had subsided and that he was beginning to see himself differently. He started question-ing his perception that he was a failure and seeing that maybe he wasn't as bad as he'd originally thought. He came to understand that his self-imposed judgement was merely a way of trying to compensate for the disappointments he had experienced in life.

I experienced another example of the power of forgiveness in working with Rose, who came to see me suffering from feelings of guilt and shame. Her history started when she born as an illegitimate child to Catholic parents in Scotland in the 1950s. She was made aware from an early age that her arrival in the world was unwelcome, and as a child was made to work long hours on the family farm and constantly criticised for her efforts. This caused her to feel undermined and unvalued, and that whatever she did was not good enough. As an adult Rose never felt worthy of her success. She overcompensated by giving her power away in relationships and work but then came away feeling used and abused.

To heal these deep patterns she worked extensively with self-forgiveness as a healing aid. She launched into working on a 'forgiveness diet'. This consists of writing the affirmation 'I forgive myself completely' 70 times a day for seven days. This is in line with a passage in the Bible in which Jesus tells Peter we should forgive our brother 70 times seven. You can either write 35 affirmations in the morning and 35 in the evening, or all of them in one sitting. It can be valuable to work with a response column to help weed out any resistance you may have to forgiving yourself completely. By using this technique Rose transformed her life and relationships. She began to discover her feelings of self-worth and to start focusing on what she really wanted in life.

For many years she had worked hard in the nightclub business, making other people wealthy. Her dream had been to own a club with a female business partner. I shall always remember the session in which she declared her desire to me. That very same evening she received a phone call from a lady offering her joint partnership in a club. One month later she was the proud owner of her own business. Rose said that to let go of her feelings of guilt through forgiveness was the crucial step towards receiving the business opportunity of her dreams.

The Path of Self-Acceptance

Everything in life that we really accept undergoes a change. *Katherine Mansfield*

One of the greatest paradoxes I have discovered in studying the process of personal transformation is that often the way to bring about change lies in our total acceptance of the very thing we want to change. Therefore if your desire is to change yourself the starting point is to accept yourself. When you fully accept yourself you surrender to who you are. Surrendering is an act of compassion by which you choose to make peace with yourself. The ego can be divisive by getting you to think that acceptance is a form of resignation or a passive state. Nothing could be further from the truth. Real self-acceptance is proactive. It is the choice to acknowledge your intrinsic worth, free from any conditions that you normally place upon yourself. Self-acceptance states that your worth is independent of what you achieve, accumulate or earn. Your true worth is inherent in your 'being'.

By receiving acceptance we come to accept ourselves

It can be difficult to relate to the idea of accepting yourself. We have become conditioned to regard self-criticism as constructive feedback so we are reluctant to let it go. Sometimes it is only through experiencing acceptance from others that we learn to accept ourselves. The first time I went to a therapist was a profound experience of receiving total acceptance. It was truly healing to be able to reveal my deepest fears and hurts and to receive acceptance in return. The therapist did not say very much in those early sessions. In this embryonic state I was able to let go and make peace with past conflict.

Happiness and self-acceptance go hand in hand

As you learn to accept yourself you open yourself to happiness. At The Happiness Project (a training programme for the promotion of happiness in all walks of life, that I co-direct the Robert Holden) the number 1 principle is, 'Unless you are happy with yourself, you will not be happy with what you do, where you are, who you are with and what you have.' The key to being happy with yourself is to accept yourself fully.

One major block to self-acceptance is the fear that if we accept ourselves then we will not improve and get on in life. I was driven by this fear for many years. I wanted to improve myself in order to feel good about myself. I attended each seminar and training session in the hope that I would reach a new level of self-improvement. I always fell short of my expectations, which led to disappointment.

Another barrier preventing us from being willing to receive acceptance is self-sacrifice: the belief that we have to sacrifice ourselves in order to be a 'good' person. This leads to the behaviour of martyrs who suffer and struggle in the name of 'doing good'. It results in feelings of exhaustion and resentment, since the martyr gives out of a sense of guilt, not joy. When we give out of guilt we are in a state of fear, which removes us from our true selves. Real giving comes from acceptance and love. Becoming aware of the areas in your life where you sacrifice, such as your relationships, at work or the way you treat yourself, enables you to make new choices.

I once counselled a lady called Pauline whose entire life appeared to be a form of self-sacrifice. She felt victimised at work in that she played the role of care-taker, trying to sort out other people's problems for them without taking care of her own needs. She led a solitary life going home at the end of each working day to shop and cook for herself. She suffered loneliness and isolation and believed that she had failed as a human being. Pauline described herself as a very giving person. She felt that she gave large amounts of love to her family but that it was not re-ciprocated: they always perceived her as fine and strong and capable of looking after herself.

When we looked at the dynamic of sacrifice, Pauline became aware that she never allowed herself to receive. She had become fiercely independent, which was a façade covering feelings of insecurity and the fear of rejection. She confided that her deepest desire was to be fulfilled in her work and to have a loving husband and children. In order to achieve these things she had to learn to receive love and acceptance. She discovered that she believed she was unworthy of receiving, which kept her stuck in the pattern.

I gave her the exercise of writing a letter to herself. I suggested that she start by writing down the reasons why she believed she couldn't accept herself. She discovered that it was her level of non-acceptance and self-hatred that fuelled the habit of sacrifice. As she kept writing with the intention of accepting herself she moved to a place of forgiveness where she was able to let go of her previous pattern of thinking. She was then able to accept herself unconditionally.

Another exercise that Pauline found useful was to write down the things that she liked about herself. She found this very challenging at first. She explained that it felt artificial and that she didn't believe what she was writing, but she was willing to do it anyway. We then discussed how Pauline could be kinder to herself to reinforce the self-acceptance. She started going to a health sanctuary, where she could feel nurtured. She then began to ask her family for support, which was a big step forward in ending her independence. Pauline continues to remind herself daily of the importance of accepting herself and she enjoys a greater degree of peace now that she no longer lives in a state of sacrifice.

The following steps are designed to encourage self-acceptance:

1. Write a letter to yourself for the purpose of healing and releasing any judgements or forms of sacrifice. Make the mental shift to forgiveness, where you are willing to forgive yourself for the way you have felt and treated yourself in the past. The ending should be a declaration of your commitment to accept yourself.
2. Give yourself a break! Talk to yourself with kindness, treat yourself with kindness, reward yourself for being you. This may feel awkward or artificial at first as you relate to yourself in a different way. Stick with it. If guilt arises from the belief that you do not deserve to be kind to yourself, learn to smile at it. It is just the ego's way of trying to keep you in sacrifice.
3. Practise mirror work. When you look in the mirror what do you see? Your beauty, radiance and

innocence, or your judgements about yourself? Spend one minute each day looking at yourself in the mirror and telling yourself that you accept yourself. Run through all the parts of your body, accepting each one. For example, 'I accept my hair', 'I accept my eyes', 'I accept my chest', 'I accept my legs', etc. Each time you feel a judgement surfacing, smile and focus on self-acceptance. Just your act of willingness to do the exercise will be a healing experience.

4. Write on different cards the statement 'I accept myself unconditionally'. Put these cards in different places as reminders – in your bag or wallet, on the car dashboard, bathroom mirror, fridge door or in a drawer in your desk. We all need constant reminders.

5. Extend acceptance to others. By accepting others you accept yourself. When you judge others you judge yourself. The next time you walk into a room of people, notice the judgements that you make. Not only does this keep you separate from others but it is your way of defending yourself from the fear of being judged yourself. Consciously choose to accept people in the room and notice how it feels. Your heart will open and you will feel connected and safe.

Ending Comparisons

In all the world, there is no one else like me. *Virginia Satir*

The family therapist Virginia Satir captures the essence of our uniqueness as human beings. She points out that everything we think, say and do is authentic because we alone choose it. Yet even though we may know that there is no one else in the world like us, we succumb to the temptation of comparing ourselves to others. It is this type of comparison that is the root cause of many of our feelings of low self-esteem and confidence. Whatever stage of life you are in, there will be people who appear lesser and greater than you. Comparing yourself to apparently lesser people will temporarily raise your esteem, whereas comparing yourself to apparently greater people will temporarily lower your esteem. Either way, comparing yourself to others disempowers you and removes you from your true self.

Common examples of comparison include comparing your relationship, work status, financial position or lifestyle to those of others.

Watch out for the 'grass is greener' syndrome

It is easy to fall into the 'grass is greener' syndrome. You believe that your life would be better if you had a different relationship, a new job, more money or lived in a different environment. When you do this you temporarily remove yourself from a position of personal power, which lies in the present moment.

Recently I played tennis with a new partner. When I told him about my work at The Happiness Project he described himself as a happy person. I asked him what contributed to his happiness and he replied, 'Not comparing myself to others.' He described it as like a game of tennis: you go back and forth always wanting to win, but whenever you do win, you start worrying about your next match. There is no peace of mind and no lasting joy.

To break the habit of comparison it is important to start appreciating your uniqueness and personal qualities. This is where true self-esteem lies, in valuing yourself now. If you find it embarrassing to focus on the qualities that make you unique, this is a healthy sign because it means that you are moving out of your comfort zone. Appreciating your strengths and qualities makes it easier for other people to appreciate you. Otherwise you will tend to deflect compliments because you do not believe that you are worthy of receiving them.

Reflect on the following statements, which are aimed at helping you to reposition yourself in your own mind:

What I like about myself is . . .
What I value about myself is . . .

What I appreciate about myself is . . .
My strengths are . . .
The way I contribute to others is . . .

Lightening Up!

Angels can fly because they take themselves lightly. *G. K. Chesterton*

The ability to be playful and light gives you a healthy sense of perspective in life. It shifts you away from being too self-absorbed and enables you to rise to the challenges you meet. As the old saying goes, 'Those who can laugh at themselves will never cease to be amused!' The trouble is that we have learned to take ourselves so seriously that we perceive it as an irresponsible act if we lighten up and laugh at ourselves.

One of the first questions I ask people to consider in a workshop is, 'Do you want to be the type of person who lights up a room when you walk in, or when you walk out?' In surveys one of the qualities that people find most attractive in others is a sense of humour. This does not mean that you have to be a stand-up comic, but developing the capacity to lighten up is a good place to start.

When in the darkness study the light, not the darkness.

The great gift humour offers is to encourage you to look at yourself in a different light. If you have identified strongly with the negative beliefs of the ego, it is a healing experience to look for the joy within.

I worked with a lady called Mary, whose ability to lighten up about herself proved to be the turning point in her journey. She had experienced the divorce of her parents when she was a child and she had vowed that this would not happen to her own children. When Mary discovered that her husband had left her for another woman it was a devastating moment. She had two young children and her greatest fear was being realised. When she allowed the fear to take over, all she could do was blame herself and judge herself for being a useless mother and wife. This left her feeling hopeless and unable to function. The pressure was on since she had to look after the children, who were behaving in a difficult manner following their father's betrayal.

In one session Mary experienced a breakthrough when for no apparent reason she started to laugh. This released a tremendous amount of tension and fear from her system and enabled her to have a new perspective. For the first time she stopped blaming herself for the separation and began to see how well she was coping. She recognised her devotion to the children and saw how her own experience could help them. She found that as she went home in a lighter mood, it rubbed off on them and they were able to start rebuilding their life with a feeling of hope and optimism.

To become more light-hearted commences with the willingness to see yourself differently. Groucho Marx demonstrated that lightness never abandoned him, even in the midst of serious illness. He was in his late eighties, in hospital, when a nurse came up to him and started talking about her fear of never getting married. She said, 'Oh Groucho, I'm going to wind up an old maid.' Groucho immediately replied, 'Well bring in another one, and we'll wind them up together!'

The key to lightening up is to accept yourself. Once you take a few steps toward self-acceptance, you begin to notice that you smile more and judge less.

Being Authentic

When you are true to yourself, you experience real self-esteem. The extent to which you deny your authentic self is the extent to which you experience inner turmoil. Being authentic can feel risky if you are accustomed to playing roles and wearing different masks in life. But ultimately you will be surviving close encounters of the stressful kind, rather than thriving on encounters of the joyful kind, by not being true to yourself.

In my early twenties I was in America on a training programme for seminar leadership. One of the exercises was to present material to our peers, who then gave us feedback. If you have ever received constructive criticism from your colleagues then you know that it can be a near-life experience! I was doing well until someone said that they felt I was being a chameleon. I shrugged it off because in my eyes I was being honest and open and if they couldn't see that, then it was their problem! But the comment stayed with me and I couldn't get rid of the feeling that maybe I wasn't being as authentic as I thought. I reflected deeply on the observation and came to realise that I had become so good at putting on a mask and appearing as I believed others wanted me to be, that I had lost my real self. In the end I was grateful for the feedback, because although it had caused me initial dis-comfort, it moved me towards being my authentic self.

There is a temptation to sell out on your authentic self in order to try and have outer success. You conform to the images that you see in magazines and advertising campaigns to give you a sense of belonging. In work you compromise yourself in order to feel accepted, and in your relationships you put on an act so that people will like you. I often hear people arguing that it is not possible to be yourself, but there are some inspiring examples of people who are. World leaders such as Mahatma Gandhi, Martin Luther King, Nelson Mandela and the Dalai Lama have created shifts in power through their authenticity and commitment to their beliefs. You don't have to be a world leader to be authentic, but you will become a leader in your world when you are true to yourself.

The danger of playing roles is that you can lose a sense of your own genuine self. You begin to feel disconnected from your heart and soul and it may seem that you are living somebody else's life. Tell-tale signs that you are caught in this dynamic include feeling emotionally dead, exhausted and drained; appearing tense, edgy and defensive around people; stopping enjoying your life and feeling as if you are just going through the motions.

If you experience these symptoms then it is time to rediscover your authentic self. This is an enlightening process that will help you to feel alive, fulfilled and confident. It is like peeling the layers of an onion: at the core is the real you and during the peeling some tears might be shed as you reconnect with who you really are.

I have witnessed many people's lives change for the better as they commit to being more honest and real. One client called Keith had become unhappy in his work. He had taken on a job with the understanding that he would become marketing director in two to three years. When the time came for this opportunity to be realised the other directors stalled and wouldn't fulfil their earlier promise. Although Keith was in a well paid position he felt he was not following his truth by staying. He chose to resign even though he did not have another job to go to. Leaving gave him the space to discover what he really wanted to do. He decided that his future lay in opening his own business. It was not easy for him at first but by staying true to himself he built up a thriving marketing company.

Clare was a client whose dream was to be a full-time journalist. She was doing some freelance writing on a part-time basis and was supplementing her income by doing temp work that she didn't enjoy. After much soul searching she finally summoned the courage to say yes only to journalistic work. She had great fear about where the work would come from and whether she would be able to pay the bills. She put her ideas together and sent them to editors with whom she wanted to work. Slowly but surely the offers started to come in. Eventually it reached the point where she received so many offers that she had to turn some down so that she could keep a balance in her life!

Sue was another shining example of the power of being authentic. She came to see me while commencing a painful divorce. Following betrayal by her husband she was left with intense feelings of rage and humiliation. Sue had struggled for many years trying to be true to herself in the marriage and she felt that she had sacrificed herself in order to try and please her husband. She was determined that from now on she was going to be authentic in her life. Six months after the separation she left her demanding and stressful job in the City because she could no longer tolerate the long hours and exhaustion. She had been trying to do the right thing as opposed to doing what was right for her. She realised that her dream was to go and live in Israel, which was where her heart lay. This was a big step for Sue, since it meant moving away from her grown-up children and the familiarity of England. She entered an immigration programme that took six months to complete, learning the language and immersing herself in the culture. Although there were initial difficulties in making such a transition, the fact that she was living authentically meant that she experienced a sense of peace and relaxation that she thought she had lost for ever.

Think about the areas of your life in which you feel you could be more authentic. Whether it's in your personal relationships, work or general lifestyle, having the courage to identify those areas is a big step forward. This does not mean that you have to change your life in one fell swoop. The most effective change comes from the inside out, so that as you become more genuine your life will change accordingly.

The key to being authentic is to listen and follow your intuition, which guides you to make the right decisions and to take the right actions. Being honest with yourself sets you free. As a friend said to me once, 'If you don't want to break your arse in life, then don't!' If you are wearing masks to get ahead in life you will not experience the fulfilment you seek. Removing the masks reveals your true self for the benefit of everyone.

Choosing to Love Yourself

If in one day, one hour, everything could be arranged at once, the chief thing is to love. *Fyodor Dostoevsky*

To live in the Higher Self is to make the choice to love yourself. This is a conscious decision that we need to make on a regular basis, since our commitment to loving ourselves is tested by the challenges of life. One morning I woke up feeling slightly depressed. No incident had caused me to feel this way, although Leeds United had lost the previous night! I decided to go for a jog to ease me into the day. While jogging I realised that my feelings were due to judgements I had about myself. I was caught in the ego mind and found myself having thoughts such as, 'I'm not good enough' and 'I am not achieving enough'. Once I noticed this slip from my Higher Self I resolved to change it by choosing to love myself.

Arriving home I felt lighter and clearer. I dropped my wife Veronica off to go to work and then I stopped to pick up some paint for the house. Within 60 seconds of parking in what I believed to be a legitimate space, I received a parking ticket. Then when I arrived home the paint fell over in the car, the lid flew off and white paint went all over the front seat! I had two ways to go. Either I could condemn myself and use it as evidence to show that I was not good enough. Or, I could see it as an opportunity to strengthen my commitment to loving myself and to learning how to keep a paint pot upright!

Often when we are at a turning point where we can choose love over fear, our lives seem to be in a state of chaos. As we commit to seeing the truth about ourselves the world seems to offer us plenty of opportunities to return to our old ways of thinking. Justine came to see me at a time of major change. She had been running her own company, which had failed to pick up a single contract in nine months. The business had previously enjoyed success and she was baffled. Her company was on the verge of going into receivership and she was looking for investors but felt ambivalent about taking the next step.

Justine had recently met a man who lived in Europe and they had fallen in love. The relationship felt absolutely right, but his business was at a crucial stage and needed his time and attention. There did not seem to be an obvious solution. She talked to a family member who felt that if she stayed and got investors for her company the business could be worth £2–3 million in two years and that she would be crazy to leave now after putting in so much effort. Upon reflection, Justine felt that her passion had left the business. The idea of spending the next two years turning the company around felt like a prison sentence to her. Even the prospect of creating that amount of money held no appeal.

When we looked at what the company symbolised for her she said that it was the need to be liked, to receive approval and to work hard, which had driven her for many years. Now suddenly she had a choice. She had a relationship that gave her love, peace, friendship and support. She was torn between the two. I encouraged her to see that the real choice lay within herself and that it was time to follow her own heart. She had always perceived herself as not good enough and had relied on other people and her achievements to give her the esteem that she was looking for. Justine realised that the decision needed to be based on the choice to love herself. Following that decision she finally sold the business and moved to live with her future husband.

To love ourselves is a great act of courage. Most of the messages we receive from the world are against giving love to ourselves. The ego interprets self-love as arrogant, selfish and self-centred. It convinces us that we do not deserve to love ourselves. It tells us that we are not good enough, that we haven't done enough and that we haven't suffered enough. The word 'love' has almost become a four-letter word. It is what everyone yearns for most in life and yet we place such barriers in the way of receiving it.

I watched a documentary about the life of a famous pop musician. This lady had recently left a highly successful band and she was rebuilding her career and life. The overriding message was that despite all the fame, fortune and outer success, she still craved love and never felt good enough. You could watch the pain that she experienced as she compromised her true self by trying to win the approval of others. Here was a classic example of someone striving to be loved by the world before giving love to herself.

When your motivation for doing something is governed by the need to be loved by others, it is a sure recipe for ending up disappointed. When you truly love yourself you no longer need to search for love outside yourself. The choice to love yourself heals fear and connects you with your Higher Self.

I am aware that it is easy to tell you to love yourself, but the act of loving yourself can be quite a different matter. The following guidelines are designed to help you to do this.

Having the desire to love yourself
Inherent in having a desire is the mechanism for the fulfilment of it. Rather than getting caught up in *how* to love yourself, focus on the desire for it. See if you can remember a time when you deeply

desired something and it materialised. Obviously there are certain wishes that can be instantly fulfilled, e.g. eating an ice-cream, calling a friend, reading a book. There are other desires that take great care and patience to nurture and develop, e.g. writing a book, studying a language, accomplishing a project. Here the planning, preparation and involvement strengthen the desire. So the more involved you become with loving yourself, the more your desire is strengthened.

Consciously deciding to love yourself

All change starts with making a decision. The act of deciding to love yourself shifts your focus away from self-judgement and towards being kind to yourself. Deciding to love yourself is where your personal power lies. Nobody else can make this decision for you. People can encourage you, books and seminars can give you information, but at the end of the day the decision lies in your hands.

Asking for help

It is important to share your desire with people who are going to support you. Get them to check in with you to see how you are doing. It is helpful if you can find a 'buddy': someone who is also prepared to commit to loving themselves. In this relationship you can share your reflections and feelings as you strengthen your love for yourself.

Focusing on what you already love about yourself

What is more common for you – to focus on what you love about yourself, or what you don't? Most of us have been conditioned to look for what we don't like about ourselves, in the hope that we will correct it. You may experience discomfort when you start focusing on what you *do* love about yourself: for example your smile, compassion for others or sense of humour.

Remembering to practise forgiveness

Whenever you slip back into non-loving thoughts about yourself, choose to forgive yourself. Forgiving yourself is a prescription for self-love. By forgiving, you give forth your love.

Committing to self-acceptance.
When you accept yourself you love yourself. Acceptance is the willingness to stop fighting with yourself and to surrender. You will experience relief, you will feel at peace and you will feel healed. Think of the way people treat their pets. Their pets can do no wrong and they accept their pets unconditionally. Treat yourself as you would your favourite pet: nurture yourself, cherish yourself and accept yourself.

Being kind to yourself
When do you catch yourself being hard on yourself? We are often so hard on ourselves that if we treated anyone else in the way we treat ourselves we wouldn't have many friends! Being kind means listening to yourself and honouring how you feel. For example if you are feeling weary and tired give yourself a rest. If you need some support, ask a friend for a listening ear.

Giving love = receiving love
As you give love to yourself you will naturally give love to others, and as you give love to others you will receive love from others. The belief that self-love is selfish is a mistake. Self-love is selfless because it means that you have more love to give. In a world full of suffering, pain and tragedy there is no greater gift than your love. Love heals, therefore the love you have for yourself is a healing force in the world.

The Next Step

In order to realise your true self it is essential to be emotionally strong. This provides the foundation for managing conditions such as the stress, anxiety and depression which are so prevalent in modern society. The following chapter gives you the awareness and tools to develop your emotional wellbeing. Integrating this with your new sense of self will give you greater confidence to move forward in your life.

2

Emotional Wellbeing

Life can feel like an emotional rollercoaster where we're going up one minute only to come plummeting down the next. We yearn for emotional equilibrium but find it hard to come by. Certainly in my therapeutic work, one of the greatest challenges I have observed in people is coming to terms with their emotional self. We have been raised in a culture that is afraid of emotional honesty (being self-aware and honest about our feelings) and this has stunted our growth towards fully functional adulthood. Most problems have their roots in emotional conflict, and if this can be resolved the problem falls away. I believe that addictions such as alcoholism, smoking, narcotics, gambling and workaholism are heavily influenced by our emotional state and that through emotional healing the addictions are resolved. Many relationship conflicts are also the result of unresolved personal emotional patterns. When these are resolved, peace returns to the relationship.

Our natural emotional state is one of harmony and wellbeing. Whenever you are not experiencing emotional wellbeing it is a call to reflect on yourself. When I felt angry I used to get annoyed with myself for feeling angry. This only increased the intensity of the original anger rather than letting it go. I now see anger as an opportunity to learn and to grow and perceive it as a warning light telling me that I am out of balance.

In focusing on your emotional wellbeing, it is important to recognise your genetic inheritance and temperament. By bringing these into the equation you develop greater compassion for why you feel the way you do. For example my wife Veronica has a very balanced disposition, which enables her to be in a genuinely good mood most of the time. I have a more turbulent makeup and experience a greater range of moods in the same time-frame. Learning to understand and accept our differences has been valuable for the development of our relationship.

However, temperament is not our emotional destiny. Given the nurturing and guidance that cultivate emotional skills, a shy child can grow into a more confident adult and a frightened child can learn to be calmer. Our emotional capacities are not unalterable, and with the right learning they can be developed. This is a message of hope for those who suffer from emotional discomfort. Even if we have left our childhood many years ago, we can be proactive in the development of our emotional wellbeing.

Emotional Healing Is Possible

Our healing lies in seeing that we *can* influence our mood by the choices we make in response to our feelings and that this process can help us a great deal in the way we approach life and move with it rather than against it. From my own personal experience I have discovered that there are four main steps in emotional healing:

Self-Awareness. The ability to recognise your feelings as they arise means that you can respond to them in conscious and creative ways. Inability to observe your feelings results in reactive and inappropriate responses.

Emotional acceptance. The ability to accept your feelings gives you emotional freedom. Rather than judging them as positive or negative, you are able to learn and grow from them, which increases your emotional literacy. Refusal to accept certain feelings perpetuates any discomfort experienced.

Releasing emotional patterns. An emotional pattern is a repetitive feeling that is unresolved from the past. Such feelings influence your behaviour, which impacts on your relationships and life. Releasing emotional patterns means that you are able to respond to events in life-enhancing ways.

Emotional confidence. Having the capacity to choose feelings contributes to your success. For example the development of empathy and compassion in relationships, motivation at work and joy in life.

We shall now explore each principle in greater depth.

SELF-AWARENESS

Listen To Your Feelings, They Are Telling You Something!
I have a godson called Zach, who is six years old with beautiful blond hair and big brown eyes. It is a joy to spend time with him because he hasn't stopped listening to his feelings. As a result he is naturally alive, joyous and loving. One Saturday lunch we were at my mother's house and Zach was sitting at the table surrounded by five adults. In the middle of our conversation he exclaimed, 'Can I say something, because I'm feeling left out.' He then proceeded to join in with the conversation. We all admired his self-awareness, the ability to know what he was feeling and to express it.

As an adult if you have a tendency to judge, analyse, repress, avoid, intellectualise or deny your feelings you will always be trying to do something with them. When you simply listen to your feelings you can learn and grow from them.

Feelings need feeling
The nature of feelings is for them to be felt. When you feel your feelings, they pass. When you block them, they get stuck. It always raises a smile in my workshops when I caricature an Englishman exclaiming, 'Oh my God I'm having a feeling!' The stiff upper lip that has characterised English culture ensures that we are past masters at repressing our feelings. This contrasts with the American image of 'letting it all hang out', which can lead to emotional indulgence. The middle path is to listen to your feelings, feel them and choose a loving response.

I worked with a client called Bernard who is a gifted singer/songwriter. He had produced some beautiful music but felt that he had been unable to fulfil his career potential due to feelings of fear. He resented this, which led him to take drugs and then give up his music. During his therapeutic process he became aware of the dynamic that he was caught in and chose to listen to what the fear was telling him. He learned that it was a gateway to his creativity and that if he accepted this, it could motivate him to achieve his aspirations. Rather than resenting the fear, Bernard began to welcome it. He recognised that it meant he was engaged in the creative process and as a result he could move forward with his music.

I experienced a breakthrough in to listening to my feelings when I did my first fire walk. I attended a seminar with Tony Robbins, the well-known motivational trainer. I arrived at the event with no real idea of what was going to happen. It was only when I walked in that I discovered that we were going to be walking on hot coals that first evening! Initially I panicked and wanted to leave. Thankfully my sense of curiosity (plus wanting to get my money's worth) got the better of me, so I decided to see what my feelings were telling me. The feelings of fear were representative of what was happening in my life at the time. I was starting a new business but was apprehensive about acting on my ideas. I was stuck, moving neither forwards nor backwards. After spending five hours in preparation for the fire walk, training my mental focus and learning to develop my emotional strength, I walked across the burning coals. I saw that my fear was 'excitement in disguise' and that by feeling it and doing the walk I accomplished something that at first I'd thought was beyond my reach.

Start to see your difficult feelings as warning lights on the dashboard of your car. When the lights start flashing, they are letting you know that it's time to listen to them. If you lead a busy and active life then at first you might need to schedule in time. This is the great value of personal counselling and therapy. Going to therapy is like taking your car for a service. Although it might seem to eat up precious time and money, the long-term benefit is that by maintaining the car it will give you good service. This is true of your feelings. If you don't give them the required attention then the effects can be far more costly than making the investment to raise your personal awareness.

The first time Dan came to see me, the entire session was taken up by his telling me that he didn't have the time or the money to invest in therapy. I sat and listened and by the end of the session he had becoame aware of what these feelings were telling him. He realised that as a child, whenever he wanted to tell his parents how he was feeling, they would inform him that they were too busy and didn't have the time to listen. Dan could see how he had internalised this response and was applying it to himself as an adult. As he came make his feelings a priority he recovered a sense of emotional wellbeing.

A powerful example of the importance of acknowledging feelings has been recorded in the work of Dr Bernie Siegel with cancer patients. He discovered that those who attended support groups lived on average much longer than those who didn't. It seems then that the act of being able to listen to and express feelings whilst having them listened to, is a healing in itself.

What you can feel, you can heal

Attending therapy is certainly not the only way to listen to your feelings. Keeping a feeling journal is an effective way of developing a healthy relationship with your emotional self. Devote 15 minutes each day to writing down what you are feeling. This can be quite challenging, since the analytical mind wants to edit or understand what you're putting down. It is important to write in a stream-of consciousness way, e.g. 'I'm feeling exhausted, I don't want to be writing down how I feel, it's boring . . . I want to go and turn on the television and switch off so I don't have to worry about my feelings. I don't have to worry about my feelings anyway but doing this exercise makes me feel uneasy. I don't know what I am going to find, and I'm not sure how I'm going to benefit from this. Maybe I won't like my feelings or I'll find them uncomfortable. I'm thinking about the chocolate ice-cream sitting in the fridge, maybe I should go and indulge myself, but that will only make me feel guilty! No I have to stay here and keep doing this . . .'

Keeping a feeling journal is a constructive way of discovering or recovering your emotional wellbeing. As you develop this skill you will begin to notice patterns emerging in your feelings. Maybe you have a tendency to worry a lot: whatever is happening in your life, you worry, even when there is nothing to worry about. Perhaps you have an inclination to feel guilty or to feel angry much of the time. To continue with the journal helps to flush out your emotional patterns. Some days you might find that you are feeling peaceful, joyous and happy: writing down these types of feeling is just as valid as recording the darker emotions.

When Alex first started his journal he experienced both resistance and anticipation. He wanted to develop a wholesome relationship with his feelings since in his relationships with women the major complaint he heard was that he was out of touch with them. Alex committed to writing first thing in the morning. He wrote about his dreams from the previous night, about his feelings from the day before and about his hopes and fears for the forthcoming day. He commented that the journal enabled him to rediscover his feelings. He was then able to project himself into other people's situations and to develop a greater intimacy in his relationships as his ability to be empathetic increased with his own self-awareness.

Emotional acceptance

There is no such thing as a negative feeling

I used to want to live in a permanent state of ecstasy, joy, happiness, serenity, peace and wonder. Whenever I felt emotions such as fear, anger, sadness, depression, angst or anxiety I would feel frustrated with myself and yearn to get back to more pleasant feelings. I believed these emotions to be negative. As soon as you label something negative you have placed a judgement on it. Calling an emotion negative suggests that there is something wrong with it and that you should get rid of it. I spent many years trying to get rid of my so-called negative emotions. I went to anger workshops to work out my anger and to empowerment workshops to break through my fear. After all this work, I found that I still had feelings of anger and fear. This is not to say that these workshops don't work. They just highlighted for me that there is no such thing as a negative feeling and that setting out with the intention to get rid of one is not necessarily the best way forward.

Following this revelation I then started to practise accepting my feelings. Rather than judging them as negative or positive I decided to see them differently. When you accept your emotions you apply love and forgiveness to them. This opened a window of opportunity for me which freed me from making such judgements.

The most effective way to develop the acceptance of feelings is through the practice of meditation. There is a particular form of meditation called a 'naming meditation' in which you name the feelings you encounter. By doing this you increase clarity and your understanding of them. You start to witness your emotions, thereby detaching yourself from the emotional current you are experiencing. This is especially helpful in learning to manage your difficult emotions because the act of naming them gives you power over them. In ancient cultures shamans learned that to name that which you fear is a practical way to master the fear. When you accept a fear, the energy of the fear dissipates.

Naming meditation

Begin by sitting comfortably in an upright position. Focus your mind on your breathing. With each breath silently name 'in-breath, out-breath', which gives your thinking mind a way to support awareness rather than wandering off in some other direction. Continue doing this for a few minutes until you are in a more centred state. As you continue to meditate, begin to notice any emotions that surface. For example you might start feeling anger, restlessness, boredom, tiredness, peace, joy or love. With each emotion that arises, silently name the feeling. If you become aware of anger say to yourself, 'anger, anger, anger.' When it passes return to naming the breath until another emotion becomes prominent, such as 'peace, peace, peace'.

Working with this meditation allows you to develop the capacity to accept your feelings because you are no longer directly caught in them. Picture yourself sitting by the edge of a river while your feelings float down with the current. As the feelings pass down the river you name them as you go, but you don't jump in to catch each feeling. Another helpful way to encourage the acceptance of your feelings is to start saying that you are *with* a feeling rather than that you *are* the feeling. This has its roots in the Buddhist tradition. Buddha's instruction on mindfulness directed meditators to note, 'This is a mind filled with joy', or 'This is a mind filled with anger'. I suggest to clients that rather than saying, 'I am angry', or 'I am happy', they should say, 'I am with anger', or 'I am with happiness'.

Gordon was a client who upon awakening each morning would feel angry. It would completely colour his outlook and send him into the day feeling resentful, tense and frustrated. He had tried many different anger management techniques: he went for jogs, took cold showers and wrote down his feelings. He was working hard at it but even though they were all good ideas, the anger persisted. Finally he admitted that since he identified himself as an angry person, it had became a self-fulfilling prophecy.

We discussed the idea of naming the anger. His commitment was simply to watch the anger and silently say, 'anger, anger, anger'. At first Gordon found this extremely challenging since the temptation to slip back into seeing himself as angry was so strong. By being patient and sitting quietly in the morning watching the anger he developed a sense of acceptance within. He began to see the anger as an old acquaintance whom he no longer needed. As he detached himself more and more from the anger he noticed that it no longer troubled him.

You are not your feelings

You are not your feelings. In other words you have your feelings but they do not define who you are. If you are feeling angry it doesn't mean that you are an angry person; equally if you are feeling depressed it doesn't mean that you are a depressed person. Describing your feelings in this fashion brings a healthy detachment, enabling you to relate to them in a different way. Saying that you are *with* a feeling symbolises your acceptance of it while at the same time acknowledging that you have a choice about how you relate to it. Either you can perceive an emotion as a friend and be kind to it, or you can view it as an enemy, in which case you attack it or defend yourself from it.

Keeping breathing!

The breath is the most powerful physical tool you have to create emotional wellbeing. In *Molecules of Emotion*, Candace Pert explains that there is a wealth of data showing that changes in the rate and depth of breathing produce changes in the quantity and kind of peptides that are released in the brain. Many of these peptides are endorphins, the body's natural painkillers, which are released rapidly in an attempt to restore and maintain emotional balance when we take deeper and more relaxed breaths.

Breathing deeply when you are faced with heightened emotional intensity allows feelings to flow through you. I wish that I had known this when I was a musician. Before each concert adrenalin would pump through my body, causing me to feel afraid and interfering with my memory and performance. Now when I give presentations I still experience the release of adrenalin, but I have learned to breathe deeply, thereby harnessing the energy to add to my concentration and focus. I still get nervous but I am no longer afraid of feeling nervous. I accept the nervousness as a natural part of performing and turn it into a welcome benefit.

There are many occasions when breathing consciously lends a helping hand. For example, if you are going out on a date the emotions can be running high. As you worry about what to wear, what to say and what's going to happen, breathing deeply helps your emotions stay level. When you go for a job interview, breathing deeply helps you to keep a clear mind when there might be anxiety or apprehension. If you are afraid of flying, breathing consciously upon taking off, regularly during the flight and when landing can help ease the pressure.

The four basic components for relaxed, deep breathing:

1. Take a deep breath in through the nose, then breathe out from the bottom of your lungs, feeling your abdomen rising, and exhaling through the nose in an even rhythm until you feel your abdomen fall.
2. Breathe slowly, taking 6–8 breaths a minute.
3. Listen to the breath coming in through the nose and exhaling through the nose.
4. Repeat for 1–3 minutes, or indefinitely.

Practise this type of breathing twice a day until it becomes second nature for you to breathe deeply and in a relaxed way.

Developing the silent witness

> In truth it is life that gives unto life – while you, who deem yourself a giver, are but a witness. *Kahlil Gibran*

The silent witness is the aspect of you that watches your life, as if it were a movie on a screen. People who have had out of body or near death experiences recount how they observed their body, mind and emotions without being 'in' them.

As you are reading now, see if you can become aware of a presence that is noticing yourself reading this book, thinking your thoughts and feeling your feelings. This presence is your witness. It is detached from your emotions, thinking and behaviour. Now begin to notice things about your life. Notice how relaxed you feel, or how much tension you have. Notice your physical appearance, how good you feel about your body and your energy level. Notice how you use the time in your life, how much time you spend at work, with your family, playing and with yourself. As you focus on noticing you become aware of the silent witness who is doing the noticing. This is an aspect of your awareness, which is always available to you. The main quality of the witness is compassion. It brings love and understanding to all areas of your life. So as you notice your emotions more you develop a greater level of compassion for them.

This is certainly very helpful when you are 'stuck' in old emotional patterns such as depression, anxiety, anger or guilt. As you become aware of the witness observing these emotions you stop identifying so strongly with them and realise that you are more than your feelings and sensations. You have created some breathing space between you and your feelings, which helps you to accept them.

This too shall pass!

One of the sayings which helps me most to cope with feelings is, 'This too shall pass.' The irony is that when you are having a pleasant feeling such as happiness, peace or relaxation you know only too well that this will pass. But when you are experiencing depression, anxiety or anger you think that they will last for ever. You cannot remember having felt good in the past and you cannot picture yourself feeling good again in the future. Your perception collapses, stimulating feelings of uncertainty and doubt, which add to the discomfort. Reminding yourself that 'This too shall pass' is a wake-up call when you are in emotional pain. It also allows you to make peace with your feelings rather than to be in conflict with them. It is a sign that you trust that they will change and that you can afford to let go of the effort involved in trying to control them.

Releasing emotional patterns

I can't express anger. I grow a tumour instead! *Woody Allen*

We all have our favourite ways of releasing our emotions. For some it is a workout in the gym, for others it is a chat with a friend, and for others a night out on the town blows away the cobwebs. These can be effective ways of releasing emotions in the short term but for long-term wellbeing it is essential to have resolved emotional patterns. The most common patterns that I have witnessed are struggle, guilt, fear, anger, depression and stress. These influence our entire lives and in some cases cause a person to be unable to function in healthy ways.

There is now evidence to suggest that there is a direct connection between emotions and physical health. This field is called psychoneuroimmunology, or PNI, and is now a leading-edge medical science. It looks at the links between the mind and the immune system. In *Emotional Intelligence Daniel* Goleman presents evidence that supports this connection:

> People who experienced chronic anxiety, long periods of sadness and pessimism, unremitting tension or incessant hostility, relentless cynicism or suspiciousness, were found to have double the risk of disease – including asthma, arthritis, headaches, peptic ulcers and heart disease.

Releasing unhealthy emotional patterns requires patience and a commitment to your happiness and wellbeing. Many of these patterns are rooted in your childhood experiences and have been reinforced over the years by your belief systems and expectations. By applying the following ideas you will begin to experience the healing that results from resolving past emotional patterns.

Ending the struggle

To many people, life can seem a struggle but, whereas life *does* involve effort, there is a big difference between effort and struggle. Effort is the result of a desire and applied focus to achieve our desires. Struggle is effort laced with fear and desperation, causing us to feel as if we are continually swimming against the tide.

Let's take a look at where this notion of struggle comes from. As a child you probably received messages such as; 'Life is a struggle', 'It is noble to struggle' and 'You achieve great things by struggling'. You may have seen your parents struggling in their own lives, either in their relationship, at work, financially or in trying to raise you. You may well have seen struggle in your education either in teachers' attitudes, from your own learning experience, or, if you received religious conditioning, then you may have been introduced to the idea of struggle being noble and righteous.

From this background you developed the belief that the essence of life is struggle and that you have to struggle to survive. Another influential force in relation to struggle is that it can be your subconscious attempt to get the love and attention you desire. Since you received attention as a child by struggling, you believe that there is a good chance that you will get the sympathy vote now as an adult if you struggle.

How this pattern works is shown in the case of a client called Debbie. Each week she had a new collection of stories to relate, all linked to her need to struggle. It seemed as if she lived for the drama of it. When we looked into it more deeply she admitted that she was afraid to let it go. It had become such a way of life that she confessed she wouldn't know what to do if she weren't consumed by struggle. She found herself in relationships where it was a struggle to communicate, attracting men who appeared only interested in her sexually, who were already in a relationship or who lived in another country. When she did meet someone who was suitable and available she would lose interest, claiming they were boring and not her type. Debbie struggled financially, living from week to week without restraining her lifestyle according to the money she had. For her the idea of structuring it so that she didn't have to struggle financially seemed restrictive and futile. In fact this often happens to people who have become so attached to struggle that the idea of an easy, flowing life seems too threatening to handle.

Think for a moment. Where do you struggle in your life? Which are the areas where you experience greatest angst? The most common are as follows:

Your physical body.
We live in a society where there is great pressure to look a certain way. Notice if you try to live up to images you see in the media or to other people's expectations of your body. Your body is your home, so it is important to be kind to it, feed it nurturing food, exercise it with care, give it the rest it requires and treat it with massages when it needs pampering. Letting go of the struggle with your body will bring you increased energy, self-esteem and balance.

Your emotional wellbeing.
Struggle acts as a form of emotional self-punishment, linking you to feelings of guilt, unworthiness, fear and doubt. When you are struggling emotionally, practise being compassionate with yourself applying forgiveness and self-acceptance.

Your psychological state.
Struggling in your mind creates conflict, indecision and confusion. The practice of meditation is the most effective way of letting go of psychological struggle and returning to a peaceful state.

Your spiritual harmony.
One of the primary functions of the ego is to keep you struggling spiritually. The essence of spirit is peace and it is this peace that appears so threatening to the ego. When you find yourself caught in the ego, turn to spirit and ask for help to let go of the struggle.

Your relationships.
The pattern of struggle is one of the greatest causes of stress and breakdown in relationships. It creates conflict and disharmony that can become habitual. If your relationships cause you to struggle, ask yourself why. Reflect on how your attitude to relationships prevents them from being a source of support and joy. Consider the possibility of enjoying struggle-free relationships.

Your physical environment.
Are your circumstances designed to support you? Or are you at the mercy of them? Do you live in a home that is in constant need of repair so that every spare minute is taken up with DIY? Would you be prepared to pay for a cleaner if you had a full schedule and didn't have the time to do it yourself? Do you struggle with your journey to work? Can you give yourself an extra five minutes so that you're not rushing all the time? What are you willing to do to make your physical environment more nurturing and supportive?

Your work.
Bringing struggle into work is the cause of many of the problems and stresses we experience. Work can be quite challenging enough without having to struggle with it as well! A theme that is currently popular is to 'work smarter, not harder', which encourages people to be creative about the way they use their time and resources.

Your finances.
Money is the last refuge of the ego and is often the area where we project our need to struggle the most. We struggle when we have money by worrying that it's going to run out, by overspending so that it does, or by depriving ourselves of the things we want. We struggle when we don't have money by feeling unworthy of having it, helpless about getting it or jealous of those who have it. Make sure that you contain and balance your life within the financial resources that you already have and then focus on letting go of the struggle so that you can experience greater financial ease and abundance.

Letting go of struggle
To become aware of the areas in which you struggle is the first step towards letting the struggle go. At first it can be quite disconcerting because the struggle can appear to become worse. This is simply because you are noticing it so acutely.

I experienced a breakthrough in letting go of struggle while meeting two friends of mine. Once a month the three of us (who are all self-employed) met and decided to try and place our attention on 'being' rather than 'doing'. We agreed to meet on a Monday morning to play some football as a way of breaking out of the traditional struggle of the Monday morning work routine. The first time we played I wasn't sure if I was even going to stay alive as I felt so guilty at not being in the office! Given that I worked for myself and was accountable only to myself, this seemed an extreme reaction, so we extended our Monday morning sessions until they became a comfortable experience.

If you catch yourself struggling, ask yourself what you are resisting. Struggle acts as a delay in getting what you want. For example if you are struggling in your relationships, ask yourself why you are resisting love and happiness. Since struggle is a symptom of low self-esteem, you might not believe that you deserve the love and happiness you desire. If you are struggling with work, ask yourself what you are resisting in your working life. Maybe you are delaying going for a promotion or starting your own company because you are afraid that you won't succeed. The act of awareness on its own can be enough for you to let go of the resistance.

You can then choose the alternative to struggle: the principle of least effort. This is when you experience a flow in your life. Things just happen and your life just works. Whether you call this serendipity or coincidence, you know that you are in the flow because you enjoy a sense of ease and rightness about your life. When you are in the flow you become connected with your spiritual dimension. The struggle is replaced with creative energy, transforming your limited world into a world of endless possibilities. Ease becomes the barometer by which you measure your life and you welcome the idea that if something is easy for you, it is right for you.

Nature is a wonderful example of the principle of least effort. Observe yourself when in good health. Notice how your heart beats effortlessly, you breathe freely, your blood flows without strain and your body functions without conscious effort. Reflect on how birds fly gracefully, fish swim naturally, grass grows and the sun shines easily. These are all natural responses, which require no extraneous effort. It is our choice whether or not to plug into this current.

Giving up guilt

> To make mistakes is human; to stumble is commonplace; to be able to laugh at yourself is maturity. *William A. Ward*

The pattern of guilt usually stems from our childhood when we didn't feel that we could please our parents or live up to their expectations. This causes us to believe that there is something wrong with us, or that we have done something wrong. When we are adults, guilt contributes to feelings of low self-esteem, causing us to resort to comfort substitutes such as overeating, drinking and smoking. We don't believe that we are worthy of getting what we want and we often subconsciously sabotage the love and success we do receive. We give up on our dreams and creativity because we feel that we do not deserve to thrive and be happy.

Life can become dominated by prescriptions such as 'should', 'ought' and 'have to', a condition that Albert Ellis the founder of Rational Emotive Behaviour Therapy, jokingly called, 'musturbation'. A life motivated by this condition creates resentment and bitterness and you lose joy and motivation. You are driven by a fear that if you don't do what you think you 'have to' then you won't be a good person. I had a client called Barry whose life was filled with 'musturbation'. He believed that he had to please everyone in his life. As a result he was constantly doing things that he didn't want to do but felt too guilty to refuse; he was afraid of upsetting others and hurting their feelings. Suffering from a pattern of guilt causes you to have a misplaced sense of responsibility. When you are hooked into this pattern, it is valuable to remember that you have a responsibility to others, but that you are not responsible for them. Your responsibility is to be honest with others, for example by saying 'yes' when you mean 'yes' and 'no' when you mean 'no'.

Begin to notice when you start sentences with 'should', 'ought' or 'have to'. For example, 'I should work ten-hour days', 'I ought to go to the gym four times a week', 'I have to complete my "to do" list each day'. These might be things that you want to do, but when they are motivated by a sense of guilt they become a duty. By replacing 'should' and 'ought' with 'could', and 'have to' with 'want to', you become aware that you do have a choice. Tell yourself that you could work ten-hour days, that you might go to the gym four times a week and that you want to complete your 'to do' list – but that you don't have to. This undoes the guilt and allows you to be true to yourself.

I had a client called June, who suffered from the pattern of guilt. She was a working mother with two children and an elderly demanding mother. June felt as if she was juggling her life and failing miserably. She couldn't seem to please anyone. Her children were playing up, she found it difficult to communicate with her husband and her mother moaned at her on their daily phone call. She believed that she wasn't good enough. This resulted in her feeling guilty, which was like a noose around her neck. It prevented her from enjoying her work and life because she perceived herself as constantly getting things wrong. She punished herself by expecting more of herself each day. She pushed herself until suffering exhaustion or sickness in order to try and compensate for the guilt.

June had lost any sense of perspective on her life. She was playing the role of 'superwoman' while believing that she was no good. By encouraging her to appreciate what an amazing job she was doing, I got her to recognise that the real problem lay in her feeling of guilt and that by letting go of it she could refocus her life.

The effects of guilt are that you put yourself down, condemn yourself and deprive yourself of what you want. If something good does happen, you see it as just a lucky break and tell yourself that it isn't going to last since all good things are followed by a fall. You feel unworthy of having what you desire and you believe that you should always settle for second best. You don't stand up for yourself and tend to get used in relationships because you find it so hard to say no.

To check your levels of guilt, notice how you react when you see a police car in your rear-view mirror. Do you get nervous and imagine that it is coming after you? Another testing moment can be at passport control in an airport. Do you ever feel uncomfortable while going through Nothing To Declare? How do you feel when your boss shows up at work? Do you believe that he/she is going to tell you that you have done something wrong? Relating to authority figures with a sense of guilt is an indication that you are carrying it from childhood.

Here is a useful exercise to help undo guilt. At the top of a page put: *Something I feel guilty about is* . . . Writing this down helps you clear it from your system. It also enables you to distinguish between old feelings of guilt and your conscience, which is your deep inner awareness of right and wrong. The expression 'having a guilty conscience' is a source of confusion because your conscience can never be guilty. It is the voice of wisdom that makes you aware of guilt and corrects your thinking or behaviour so that you maintain your integrity. Giving up guilt clears your conscience because you let go of self-destructive habits that cause you to withdraw your love from the world.

As you release guilt you reclaim your innocence. You were born innocent and behind your guilt rests your innocence waiting for you to rediscover it. The following visualisation is designed to help you reconnect with your original purity. Have someone read it to you if you can, or record it on tape and listen to it.

Sitting in a comfortable position, close your eyes and focus on your breath. Allowing it to become slower and deeper, feel your body relaxing. In your mind's eye picture yourself as a young child. See every detail of this child, its perfect features, beautiful skin and loving eyes. Now see if you can connect with its innocence, divinity and purity. It is untouched by the world and by any outer conditioning. As you do this, become aware that this child exists within you. Tell yourself that you are innocent and that whatever has happened in your life this innocence is still there waiting for you to reclaim it. See yourself peeling away any layers of guilt so that what is left is pure love. If you experience blocks in letting go, choose to forgive yourself for past mistakes, wrong deeds and miscommunications. Holding on to guilt is not a solution. It is time to set yourself free by returning to your birthright, your complete innocence. When you are ready, take several deep breaths, open your eyes and stretch your body.

To strengthen this visualisation it is helpful to work with some of the following affirmations:

◆ I am innocent.
◆ I forgive myself for thinking I was guilty.
◆ I choose to be kind to myself.

◆ I can have compassion for others without taking on their pain.
◆ Saying 'no' when I mean 'no' and 'yes' when I mean 'yes' supports everyone.
◆ I deserve to be happy.

If you still experience blocks in reclaiming your innocence, look at the list of things you feel guilty about and be willing to make amends where necessary. Table 4 is an example of how you can do this.

TABLE 4

Guilt	Amend	Date
Owing a friend £100.	Call them up and arrange payment.	14 May
Eating chocolate.	Eat fruit instead.	7 May
Having fun.	Tell myself I deserve it and schedule in an enjoyable activity.	10 May

The journey to healing and releasing guilt is an ongoing one. It involves continued commitment to combining integrity with self-acceptance.

Freedom From Fear

It's not that I'm afraid to die. I just don't want to be there when it happens. *Woody Allen*

Do you live in a permanent state of mild fear, which causes feelings of tension, anxiety, or panic at the drop of a hat? It can seem as though the major part of our lives is run by fear. We fear failure and we fear success. We fear rejection and we fear intimacy. We fear pain and we fear pleasure. We fear loss and we fear commitment. We fear change and we fear 'staying stuck'. Fear shows up in all areas of our lives as an irrational, non-specific and destructive force. It prevents us from following our dreams and wishes and leaves us feeling drained and demoralised.

The only thing we have to fear is fear itself. *Franklin D. Roosevelt*

Fear is frightening because fear can only see itself in everything. Freedom from fear lies in willingness to change your mind about yourself. As long as you continue to believe that you are an ego then you will feel afraid. When you are connected with your Higher Self you will be able to let go of fear. There is nothing to fear in the world of the Higher Self since there is nothing it cannot handle. Depending on how you see yourself, you either experience the world as a place of fear or a place of perfect safety.

In the transition from fear to trust there are some stepping stones along the way. The first one involves a period of education. Since you learned to feel afraid in your life, you can relearn to feel safe. Psychologists call the process of learned fear, *fear conditioning* whereby something that is not threatening becomes feared, as it is associated in your mind with something frightening. By changing the association in your mind you learn to feel differently about it.

I had the experience of relearning the first time I led a public seminar. I felt absolutely terrified since I had associated public speaking with the fear of appearing stupid, making mistakes, not being liked and my future as a presenter being ruined. I was so afraid that I couldn't speak throughout most of the seminar. Thankfully I had a co-presenter that day who was happy to run the seminar while I sat next to her trying to regulate my breathing! By mid-afternoon I had relaxed sufficiently to contribute to the end of the course, which ironically was teaching about self-esteem. The lesson from this experience was that I survived. Nothing life-threatening happened and it enabled me to change my association with public speaking from one of fear to anticipation. Nowadays I experience the same energy that paralysed me on that first day, but this time it energises me.

The number one public fear is of public speaking. Yet the only way to conquer the fear is to do it, otherwise the fear gets bigger and bigger.

> It was a high counsel that I once heard given to a young person: Always do what you are afraid to do. *Ralph Waldo Emerson*

Susan Jeffers's message in the title of her bestseller *Feel the fear and Do It Anyway* sums up the process of responding to fear. You need to feel your fear and do what you want to do in spite of it. Think back to all the times you felt afraid and did it anyway and what you would have missed out on if you hadn't.

Fear forward!

As you become willing to move forward by doing what you fear, the feelings of fear diminish.

A common fear that I observe in people is that of being rejected. It is natural to want to be liked, but if you compromise yourself because of the fear of rejection, then it's time to move beyond that gear. The following story is how one teacher of mine healed his fear of rejection.

One day Bob decided that he was going to overcome his fear of being rejected by women once and for all. With this end in mind he took up a position on a street corner in New York, said 'hello' to each woman he was attracted to and invited her to go out. At first he was devastated when he was rejected and he sought solace in a cappuccino in the coffee shop next door. However, he was determined to keep going until the fear of rejection had diminished. By the second day he had become so used to hearing 'no' that it was like water off a duck's back. On the third day a new fear emerged: the fear of hearing 'yes'.

This principle is taught in sales training, where people are encouraged to welcome hearing 'no' because it means that they are getting closer to a 'yes'. If you are not getting any 'nos' then you are not out pitching for sales.

FEAR: false evidence appearing real

The above acronym is a helpful antidote when you are stuck in fear. For example, when you arrive at work, there is a message sitting on your desk from your boss requesting a meeting. Coming from fear, you immediately predict the worst and start imagining that you are going to be fired. In fact it turns out that he wants to run some ideas past you because he values your opinion. Your partner calls you at work, asking to meet with you later on. Coming from fear, your first response is to worry about why he/she wants to talk to you. You discover that evening that what he/she wants is to schedule a holiday so that you can spend more time together.

Fear can also be read as 'Forgetting Everything's All Right'. Freedom from fear is when you remember everything's all right. Since we need constant reminders that all is well, I recommend using the following visualisation whenever you are experiencing irrational fear.

Sitting in a comfortable position, close your eyes and focus on your breathing. Allowing it to become slower and deeper, feel your body relaxing. With each breath silently repeat 'letting go, letting go' until you have a sense of stillness and relaxation. Then in your mind's eye picture yourself free from fear. Notice what images surface in your mind and what feelings arise in your body. If you experience any resistance to this idea, gently return your awareness to your breath and repeat 'letting go, letting go'. Now say to yourself, 'There is nothing to fear.' Remember that the presence of fear is an indicator that you are trusting in the ego. The awareness that there is nothing to fear reflects your recognition of the power of the soul. Imagine your soul as a great being of love and truth. Notice how it feels to be in its presence and see if you can allow yourself to be strengthened by the power of it. The instant you are willing to do this, there is indeed nothing to fear. When you are ready, take several deep breaths, open your eyes and stretch your body.

Addicted to anxiety

Having too much fear on a daily basis means that anxiety can creep in through the back door. You start to worry about every little detail of your life, and if you catch yourself not worrying then you worry about that too! Worrying has almost become a job description for adulthood. The rational mind goes, 'If I worry enough then I am being a responsible and professional adult.' In the workplace a worrier is perceived as a warrior, fighting for a noble cause, whereas someone who is calm and relaxed is seen as a slacker. As a parent, worrying about your children is a sign that you are doing a good job and that somehow they will be assured of a good future. But has worrying ever truly solved your problems?

Maintaining a healthy perspective on life is crucial to letting go of the habit of worrying. Some of the most moving examples I have witnessed have been when working in the cancer community. You hear stories of cancer patients who say that getting the illness was the best thing that ever happened to them. They say that cancer teaches you what's important; it gives a sense of perspective so that you stop worrying about the minor everyday hassles that constantly used to irritate or upset you. When you have cancer everything else seems like 'small stuff'. This doesn't mean that nothing else matters. It's just a reminder not to let everyday problems get blown out of proportion.

As you focus on maintaining perspective, it is important not to slip into feelings of guilt if you do catch yourself worrying about small things. One tendency I have observed in clients is that they compare their problems with those who are less fortunate. They witness people in third world countries suffering horrors such as famine, poverty, drought and disease and feel guilty and ashamed. Although this is understandable it certainly doesn't help either the client or the person suffering the horror. Even though your worry is minor, feeling guilty about it only makes it worse. If you feel a desire to pledge support to those less fortunate, then do so, but don't use their plight to add to your own unhappiness.

Control freak!

Another way that anxiety manifests itself is in the desire to be in control of one's entire life. We all need a certain amount of control in order to be able to function effectively. If our life becomes too far out of control then we experience undue stress. On the other hand, being too controlling is a sure recipe for tension and high anxiety. The trouble with needing to control everything is that you miss out on the joy that comes from being spontaneous. When you are spontaneous you are open to going with the flow in life. If things don't seem to be working out in the way that you originally planned, you are able to let go and embrace the alternatives.

Man plans, God laughs!

Letting go of control is a shift in attitude, from holding a stubborn position to cultivating a flexible outlook. It doesn't mean that you don't make plans. It's just that you learn to detach from them. A helpful exercise to develop the ability to let go is to write down five ways in which you attempt to control your life and see how you can soften them. For example:

◆ *I attempt to control my life by worrying about money.*
◆ I could take responsibility for my financial situation and develop a trusting outlook.

◆ *I attempt to control my life by having a rigid schedule.*
◆ I could leave gaps in my diary for spontaneous activity.

There is a common fear that surrendering control makes you a weak person and is like waving a white flag to signal defeat. In fact, being able to let go makes you stronger and more trusting. The following Zen story illustrates the lesson of learning to let go:

Tanzan and Ekido were once travelling together down a muddy road. A heavy rain was falling.

Coming around a bend, they met a lovely girl in a silk kimono and sash, unable to cross the intersection.

'Come on, girl,' said Tanzan at once. Lifting her in his

arms, he carried her over the mud.

Ekido did not speak again until that night when they reached a lodging temple. Then he no longer could restrain himself. 'We monks don't go near females,' he told Tanzan, 'especially not young and lovely ones. It is dangerous. Why did you do that?'

'I left the girl there,' said Tanzan. 'Are you still carrying her?'

Stressed-out

If I had no sense of humour, I should have long ago committed suicide. *Mahatma Gandhi*

Technically speaking, the term 'stress' does not have the negative we associate with it. We need a certain amount of stress in life for our growth and evolution. It is when we are exposed to high levels of stress over long periods of time that the dangers of being stressed out can kick in.

One of the problems with stress is that we have developed a 'macho' response to it over recent years, a myth has grown up that the person who can handle the greatest amount of stress wins. This pattern can continue until there is a crisis, which wakes us up to the implications of long-term stress. A marriage breaks down, a health issue emerges, work commitments cannot be fulfilled or an addiction takes over. Increasing awareness of our current response to stress enables us to make any necessary changes to achieve a successful balance between work, rest and play.

I used to be caught in the 'macho' trap of thriving on stress. I was under the impression that the higher my tolerance to stress, the more effective I was. I craved a 24-hour lifestyle of action, action and more action. This continued until I found myself constantly irritable and tired, with digestive and sleep difficulties. Since then I have worked on lowering my tolerance to stress and as a result I enjoy greater energy, health and wellbeing. Stress in itself can become addictive and it can take strong willpower to wean yourself off it.

It takes honesty and courage to lower your tolerance to stress. Here are a few responses from my clients who have chosen to reset the balance in their lives: 'At first I thought I would turn into a lazy person, but having greater balance means that I do less but accomplish more. I have discovered the wisdom in the statement, less is more.' 'It was an initial readjustment to stop reacting to life as if it was an emergency. I am finally enjoying the journey as well as the breaks along the way.' 'I now have more time for the truly important things in life, my family and myself!'

It was no coincidence that while I was writing this chapter I received a call from a client suffering from high levels of stress. Kate had just had a car accident, driving into a parked car by mistake. Thankfully nobody was hurt. When she called me ten minutes after returning home, she was angry with herself, blaming herself for the accident, and confused about why it had happened. Before the accident occurred she had been thinking about her recent redundancy from work and was feeling extremely angry that her former employers had not sent the paperwork and references that she had requested two months earlier.

She admitted that this was causing her to drive more aggressively than usual. She also revealed that she was on the way to the gym but had been procrastinating about going and was therefore running half an hour late. As she was talking, Kate realised that she was criticising herself for feeling angry, believing that she should be more 'enlightened'. With encouragement she could look at the lessons to be learned from the incident. She was an independent type of person, so asking for support was a big step forward. Phoning me was her way of reaching out. She could see that asking for help in a stressful situation meant that she was able to recover more quickly than by keeping it to herself. She also recognised the need to make her physical and emotional well-being a priority.

Seeing stress as an opportunity to keep yourself in balance is a way of using it creatively. When you start feeling stressed, see it as a bell warning that it's time to check your equilibrium. In order to stay on track in your own life, make the time to listen to the wise voice within you. On courses at The Happiness Project we recommend that participants allocate a chair in their home for this purpose. This becomes their 'wisdom chair'. Allow five minutes a day to listen to your wisdom. It will tell you what you need to know at the time. If you are feeling stressed maybe you need to slow down, to focus on what's important, to reach out for support, to complete a project or to have a holiday. Allow yourself to be guided by your wisdom to help you transform your stress into wellness.

The following questions are designed to help you get in touch with your wisdom.

◆ Of the people you know who handles stress the best? What is their strategy? What choices do they make? How do they respond to other people's stress?
◆ What is the most helpful thing you have ever learned about stress?
◆ What would you teach somebody else about responding to stress?

Stressing less, smiling more

Instinctively we know that humour is good for us. Research into the healing properties of laughter show that it has many therapeutic benefits. On a physical level laughter stimulates the release of two neuropeptide chemicals: endorphins and enkephalins. Both are commonly described as the body's natural pain-suppressing agents and they impact on our general mood and behaviour. Dr Lee Berk, at Loma Linda University, California, has shown that watching a one-hour comedy video increases production of many types of T cells, including helper T cells, which strengthen the immune system. Dr William Fry of Stamford University, who has studied the potential healing properties of humour for over thirty years, has noted that laughter helps stimulate the cardiovascular and respiratory system, lowers blood pressure and aids muscular relaxation. He describes laughter as a good aerobic workout and goes so far as to say that 100 to 200 laughs a day is the equivalent to about ten minutes of rowing or jogging (*The Psychobiology of Humour*, 1982 report).

On an emotional level laughter is a powerful means of releasing pent-up feelings such as anger, fear and anxiety. Most people say they feel lighter after a good laugh, as if a tremendous weight has been lifted from their shoulders. I had a client who was experiencing great stress and strain. She found that laughter would well up in her spontaneously, and as the tears rolled down her cheeks she would feel cleansed and clearer. Laughter is infectious, so it was always a bonus to receive the benefit of her laughing bouts. People report that laughing helps put them in a better mood. This is valuable, since we are less vulnerable to the harmful effects of stress when we're feeling good.

To enjoy good humour in your life start to look for the humour in different situations. A sense of humour is very personal. As the old saying goes, 'One man's meat is another man's poison.' Finding humour when under stress is challenging, since, if you're like most people, your sense of humour abandons you right when you need it the most. But your willingness is enough to set laughter in motion and enrolling your friends, colleagues and family ensures that you have the support to keep you going.

Fight, flight or frolic!
The traditional responses to stress are to confront it or to run away from it. At The Happiness Project we recommend becoming more playful as a serious way to cope with stress. The key to getting back in touch with your sense of playfulness is fun. The challenge is that having fun can appear a lost art in a world of high anxiety and constant craziness. When we are able to have fun, it encourages us to relax and look on the bright side of life.

> **Exercise:** Write down the ten favourite ways of making yourself relax and commit to doing one next time you're feeling stressed.

Undoing anger

Do you get angry and over-react to events, blowing incidents out of proportion and often being in a bad mood? The type of anger I am describing here is anger that has become a habitual response to life. We get angry as a way to vent our spleen without taking responsibility for the consequences of our actions. This type of anger can seriously damage your health and wellbeing, as well as those around you. I have seen many people distraught and hurt by the selfish expression of misplaced anger.

It is important to distinguish the form of anger highlighted above from a natural type of anger. This can be observed in responses to injustice, inequality or abusive behaviour as well as when recovering from a loss, such as a bereavement of separation. This form of anger is closely linked to a strong sense of passion and accountability in life, which are traits recognised in fully functional human beings. This passion can become a powerful motivator for accomplishing great feats such as social reform, charity appeals and innovative projects.

The habit of getting angry is a learned behaviour, usually modelled on a parental or environmental influence. I once worked with a client called Jim who described his father as a 'rageaholic'. The family would tiptoe around him in the morning trying not to cause an upset. Everyone would breathe a sigh of relief once he'd left the house as they could then get on with their day. This scenario was repeated each evening as the father arrived home from work and invariably shouted at and ridiculed the person nearest at hand. As an adult Jim noticed that in his primary relationship he had a tendency to get angry and explosive without any valid reason. Due to his childhood experience he had the mistaken belief that it is OK to dump anger on to the person you are closest to. He described the emotion as a fire raging through a dry forest: it was out of control and damaging the very thing he valued the most.

By identifying the cause and pattern of anger Jim was able to break the habit. Since it had become an automatic response he found it a challenge at first to catch the anger before it surfaced. I encouraged him to write down what he felt angry about each morning as a way of making it more conscious. Doing this enabled him to acknowledge the feeling and prevent it from being expressed in inappropriate ways. He used other techniques such as pounding pillows, physical exercise and appropriate verbal expression to work the feelings of anger out of his body. Through letting go of habitual anger Jim began to gain a new sense of freedom. He realised that anger had closed his heart and blocked him from giving and receiving the love he truly wanted.

As he continued to reflect on his experience of anger he came to understand that it also acted as a subconscious form of protection: an attempt to shut out old feelings of hurt and pain. By placing a shield around his past distress it prevented him from developing greater intimacy in his relationship and left him feeling isolated and alone. I reminded him of a useful principle in emotional healing, which is that you are never upset for the reason you think. Although he was feeling angry in the present moment the cause was an unresolved upset from the past. By understanding this concept he could see that every upset has the potential to bring greater healing and honesty. His courage and willingness to change allowed his shell to open and the disclosure of his past upset to occur. He discovered that revealing these feelings to his partner brought them closer together and dispersed the sense of separation and aloneness that he had carried for so many years.

In working with anger it is important to be aware of the role of the ego. One of the powerful dynamics of the ego is that it would rather be 'right' than happy. In other words the ego would rather be right in its misguided judgements such as 'The world is unfair', 'People are out to get you', 'Nothing ever works out' and 'Life is a relentless struggle', than let go of these types of belief and experience happiness. As the ego is driven by never finding what it's looking for, the inevitable outcome is that you end up feeling angry and frustrated.

In the Higher Self, which sees the world from the opposite perspective, you do not experience dysfunctional anger. This is because you understand that you are not a victim of the world you see. You take responsibility for your experience of life and therefore if you do feel angry you are aware that it is the outcome of holding on to a judgement. In this context a judgement is a weapon that you use against yourself and which prevents you from experiencing greater joy and peace.

In order to resolve your angry feelings begin go relate to them as a source of information. What are they telling you? What would they have you learn? Maybe they are informing you that you are out of balance in an area of your life and that you need to re-evaluate your priorities and expectations. If you find that you finish work each day feeling angry and unfulfilled perhaps you are not following your heart and doing what you really want to do, or maybe you are not being assertive enough and are letting others dominate your decisions and behaviour. If you experience habitual anger within a relationship maybe there is unfinished business from your past or you are not being fully honest in the present. Listening to your anger in this way gives you a sense of power over it rather than letting it run your life in subconscious ways.

Acknowledging anger and learning from it enables you to express it in appropriate ways. This involves taking responsibility for your feelings and being accountable for what you do communicate. Blaming another person or situation for your feelings of anger only creates further tension, putting you into a victim mentality that stops you moving forward. When communicating these feelings I recommend that you use the following phrasing: say, 'When you did X, Y or Z I felt angry . . .' rather than saying, 'You made me feel angry about X, Y or Z . . .', which is a form of blame.

Willingness to see things differently is the ultimate key to undoing anger. Each time I am tempted to get angry in my marriage I remind myself to see Veronica differently. Projected anger distorts my vision and makes me see her as the enemy. My decision to see things differently brings me back to the truth, which is that she is my closest friend and support.

Undoing anger is crucial for your emotional wellbeing because anger can become so all-consuming as to crowd every other feeling out of your heart, making you either externally aggressive or internally bitter. The person who suffers the most at the end of the day is you. Anger keeps you separate from the world around you and puts a great strain on you. Your ability to let go of anger opens the door to pure peace of mind as you are no longer caught in the desire to be 'right' rather than happy.

Being with depression

Judy came to me suffering from clinical depression. She had been diagnosed over twenty years ago, was taking a variety of anti-depressants and had seen a cognitive therapist for several years. However she still experienced feelings of fear, anguish, sadness, tearfulness, tension and anxiety. She hated the depression. It was the number one enemy with which she fought every day. She perceived herself as a failure for having depression and believed that there must be something fundamentally wrong with her. On the outside Judy had a good life. She had a loving family, two lovely kids, a kind and supportive husband, financial security and a good network of friends. She put on a brave face to the world around her and tried to make out that she was OK, while on the inside she felt as if she was dying.

The first step I took with Judy was to encourage her to see that there was nothing wrong with her for feeling depressed. I presented to her the idea that the depression was not the problem; it was the way she was responding to it that was causing her the real pain. She found this very challenging because clinical evidence showed that she suffered from a shortage of the neurochemical serotonin, which caused an imbalance in her metabolism, and everything she had been told and read about depression had contributed to her belief that there was something wrong with her.

My approach was to help Judy see that even if she had a chemical imbalance, by learning to accept her feelings and make peace with herself she could enjoy a fulfilled and rewarding life. When we began to explore her past she revealed that she had always felt as if she had not fulfilled her potential, since she had never been able to work properly. Her self-dialogue consisted of a repetition of negative statements about herself based on this fact. She repeatedly told herself that she was not good enough as a mother, wife, daughter and person in society. She constantly told herself that she was a bad person and deserved to be punished. It appeared that the pain she felt from the depression served as an effective form of punishment, since it caused her to feel bad about herself most of the time. This dynamic lowered her self-esteem and caused her to feel worthless.

I suggested to Judy that she begin to focus on remembering how she felt as a child. I recommended that she collect photographs of herself from her childhood and to see if the girl she found fitted the picture she held of herself now. When she looked at the photos she saw a beautiful, innocent child with a zest for life. I encouraged her to imagine that child still being a part of her today. By focusing on the child within her Judy was able to start forgiving herself for the way she felt and for how she treated herself. Her feelings began to soften. Some of the hurt and resentment that she was carrying dissolved. This helped her to see that she had learned a great amount about the human condition and that by sharing it she could help others suffering from depression.

We began to explore her faith again and her connection to the spiritual dimension, which she felt she had lost over the years. She had seemed so alone with her feelings that she could not imagine that she was connected to anything. Embracing the possibility that she might be more than just a body and mind gave Judy renewed hope. Developing her spiritual awareness enabled her to focus on the compassionate witness within her that could notice the depression but was not directly identified with it. She saw that she had a choice in how she saw herself: either as a depressed person, or as a person who was having the experience of depression. Her willingness to change her mind about herself became the turning point in changing her experience of depression. She could see that she had made subconscious decisions in the past that had kept her in a certain mindset and which had not helped her cause. She began to write a new script for herself, one in which she embraced her spiritual dimension while at the same time having great compassion for what she had endured.

It has been a gradual process for Judy, flipping back and forth between identification with the depression and with her spiritual self. She has found that it is possible to feel and honour her feelings while also moving on with her life. She plucked up the courage to work at a voluntary agency, which has given her a sense of self-worth and that she is making a contribution to society. She has learned to be kinder to herself as a mother and a wife, lowering the unrealistic expectations that she had placed on herself.

I have related Judy's story in detail to illustrate that working and living with depression is an ongoing journey, but that it is still possible to lead a fulfilled and creative life. Depression is very common in today's society. A report published by Channel 4, following a documentary based on Oliver James's book *Britain on the Couch*, claims that at least one in five people in the UK will have a depressive illness at some time in their life:

> The pressure on us to succeed has never been greater. From cradle to grave, we are urged to get smart, get rich, get ahead. For those who don't make the grade – in their own eyes or those of their family and friends – life can easily take a downward spiral into depression and despair.

Resolving our relationship to success is a core element in healing feelings of depression. If we constantly place success outside our reach, setting unrealistic expectations and comparing ourselves obsessively, enviously and self-destructively to others, we corrupt the quality of our inner lives. I find it ironic that following the achievement of major goals, I have experienced periods of depression. After I purchased my first home I lost my drive and motivation. I felt listless and apathetic and had a sense that life was pointless. I had got what I thought I always wanted and then it suddenly seemed meaningless. When I first appeared on television I had a similar experience. I had always wanted to work in TV yet I remember distinctly coming off the programme and thinking 'Is that it?'

It is a powerful lesson to learn that what the world offers isn't necessarily going to solve all your problems. The world can encourage you to be happy, but it cannot make you happy. I am not saying that you shouldn't aim to achieve your goals; I'm reminding you to be aware that to pin your hopes on things that are outside you will leave you feeling empty. It is when life appears to lose meaning and purpose that we often feel depressed. Thoughts such as 'What's the point?,' 'There is no meaning', 'I can't be bothered' and 'It's all too much' tend to dominate. By staying 'stuck' in these thoughts we experience great pain, but if we can use them to work out what is real and true, we open the door to enjoying a deeply purposeful life.

Emotional confidence

Through increased awareness, acceptance and release of emotional patterns you arrive at a state of emotional confidence: you have developed the capacity to choose feelings in your relationships and life that contribute to your success, rather than subconsciously reacting to the stimuli around you. For example you are able to choose peace in response to conflict, and love in response to fear.

The following ten emotional states contribute to the development of your emotional confidence and are well worth focusing on and encouraging on a day-to-day basis.

A State of Love

> For this purpose we have been created: to love and to be loved. *Mother Teresa*

When you ask yourself the question, 'Why am I here?' what comes into your mind? The majority of people I ask give the answer, 'Love.' There is no greater healing force in life than love. There is no greater bonding force in relationships than love. There is no greater gift you can give the world than love. Love is the very essence of creation. It is the life force that propels us forward and from which great beauty is produced. The opposite of love is fear: when fear dominates we experience war, conflict, disease and disharmony. Choosing love over fear is a daily practice. Committing to this choice is an act of greatness. Imagine the impact on the state of the world if everyone chose love. Martin Luther King put it this way: 'Everybody can be great . . . because anybody can serve. You don't have to have a college degree to serve. You don't have to make your subject and verb agree to serve. You only need a heart full of grace. A soul generated by love.'

We all have the capacity to have our soul generated by love. As you continue to choose love you will be filled with love. By generating and giving love, you receive love. By choosing love you go beyond appearances and connect with something deeper and more long-lasting. Love is a universal language that requires no words. In fact words are always open to mis-interpretation. Love is the experience of oneness in life, in which you perceive no separation between you and any other form of creation.

When you give unconditional love you are connected with your Higher Self. Love is an act of giving from the very depths of your heart and soul. It is an expression of your genuine, authentic self.

A passage from *Diagrams for Living* by Emmett Fox, philosopher and scientist, captures the essence of love:

> There is no difficulty that enough love will not conquer; no disease that enough love will not heal; no door that enough love will not open.
>
> It makes no difference how deeply seated may be the trouble; how hopeless the outlook; how muddled the tangle; how great the mistake.
>
> A sufficient realisation of love will dissolve it all.
>
> If only you could love enough you would be the happiest and most powerful being in the world.

Exercise: Think about how you can love yourself and others each today.

A state of trust

To trust is to be able to let go of your fears and know that you are safe and all is well. It is to take a leap of faith into the unknown and to know that all your needs are taken care of. We already trust in many ways that we are not consciously aware of. Each time we go to sleep we trust that we will wake up the next morning with our heart still beating, lungs still ventilating and blood still flowing. Each time we eat we trust that we can digest and be nourished by the food. Each time we get into the car we trust that it will take us to our destination safely. This is an intrinsic level of trust that exists in each one of us and if we become aware of this state it expands into all areas of our life.

Unfortunately, our trust has been eroded over the years. Betrayal, hurt or separation causes us to stop trusting in relationships. We become defensive and non-committal as a form of protection if our trust has been broken. The experience of loss in life, whether it is the loss of a relationship, job or home, causes us to withdraw and shut down. The challenge of difficult emotions such as anger, anxiety or depression prevents us from trusting that peace is possible and joy is natural.

When you are able to trust in yourself, you stop looking for solutions in someone or something outside yourself and you start turning to your Higher Self for answers. To trust enables you to relax and let go because it connects you with intuitive knowing rather than wishful thinking. A passage in *A Course in Miracles* says: 'Who would attempt to fly with the tiny wings of a sparrow when the mighty power of an eagle has been given you?'

The first step is to become aware of the areas in which you already trust. Reflect on all the moments when you trusted without fully knowing the implications of your actions – a time when you were feeling depressed and yet trusted that the feelings would pass; a time when you were struggling with work and yet trusted that there would be a solution; a time when you were experiencing conflict in a relationship and yet knew that harmony was on the other side. Strengthening this awareness gives you greater honesty about the areas in your life in which your trust threshold is low. Maybe you think that you trust in your finances, until your bank account is low and then fear takes over. Perhaps you think that you are trusting in your work, until you receive a piece of criticism from your boss and you are ready to clear your desk. Maybe you think you trust your partner, until they go out for a night on their own and you picture them going off with somebody else. Being honest with yourself removes any fear that prevents you from trusting on a deeper level.

A certain amount of spiritual wisdom is required in the process of trusting – expressed in the Arab proverb, 'Trust in God and tie up your camel!' For example to trust in your health, it helps to eat healthy food, to take regular exercise and to rest well. To trust in your work, it helps to be fully committed, to be a team player and to perform to the best of your ability. To trust in your relationship, it helps to be loving, honest, compassionate and caring. To align your behaviour with your conscience enables you to trust yourself.

Exercise: If you trusted fully, how would your life be different?

A state of calm

The natural extension of trust is to relax and feel calm. When we fully trust we let go of our fears and doubts, and calm ensues. There is a common misperception that being calm is a form of laziness and that calm and success do not go together. To dispel this myth, consider Paul Wilson, author of *The Little Book of Calm*, which has sold over 4 million copies! Paul thrives in several high-stress worlds: he is chairman of a Sydney advertising agency, strategic consultant to several major corporations, director of a hospital and a father. Instead of focusing on stress he has become an authority on calm.

Paul recommends in his book, 'Think calm. Have calm thoughts. Picture calm scenes. Recall calm sounds. And guess what you'll be feeling . . .' Actively involving your senses in focusing on a specific state makes the feeling more real. By discovering which sense you have a greater affinity with, you can accelerate this. Some people are naturally more visual, others are auditory and others relate more directly through touch and feelings (kinaesthesia).

To find out whether you are more visual, listen to the words that you use. Phrases such as 'I see', 'This is how it looks to me' and 'I just can't picture myself doing that', are a clear indicator. Enjoying visually stimulating activities such as art, fashion and design means that you have a strong visual sense. If you are more inclined to be auditory then you will use phrases such as 'I hear what you are saying' and 'It sounds good to me'. Favourite activities will include listening to music and being engaged in conversation. If you are primarily kinaesthetic you will use phrases such as 'I feel that I am in touch with what you are saying', 'I sense you're not happy' and 'That resonates with me'. Popular activities include physical exercise, watching emotional films or dramatic plays and getting massaged. Discovering your dominant sense means that you can use it to help you be calm by choosing activities that nourish and relax you.

> **Exercise:** Start the day by taking three deep calm breaths. Do this whenever you feel tense or irritated.

A State of Wonder

To wonder encourages you to be curious, which makes you interested and open-minded to all things. There is never a dull moment when you wonder about life. It was the Indian poet and mystic Rabindranath Tagore who wrote, 'That I exist is a perpetual surprise, which is life' (I Won't Let You Go, *Selected Poems*, UBSPD, 1992). Wondering keeps you fresh, young at heart and vibrant.

I find it a joy to watch infants marvel at the miraculous. My tennis partner, Andy, tells me of the sheer delight his six-month-old boy gets just from observing his own hands opening and closing. He becomes even more enthralled when his father joins in and they open and close their hands together.

I heard a cancer patient tell of the joy that she receives from lying outside with her daughter, looking up into the sky and wondering at the trees, the birds and the clouds. People frequently say that it is the simple things in life that make the difference and that bring true joy.

When you are fearful or stressed you are removed from the joy of wonder and your wondering turns to whether you will feel normal again and whether the pressure will ever stop. At these times it is valuable to stop your life for a moment and wonder at the miracle of just being alive.

> **Exercise:** Stop for a moment each day and wonder at this opportunity called life.

A state of adventure

> Life is either a daring adventure or nothing. To keep our faces towards change and behave like free spirits in the presence of fate is strength undefeatable. *Helen Keller*

To wonder leads us to capture the spirit of adventure. The capacity to see your life as a journey that unfolds with unlimited potential connects you with this state. I find it fascinating to observe people make an adventure of their lives. Richard Branson is an inspiring example. His business appears to be a never-ending source of adventure, and his hot-air balloon attempts symbolise his desire to rise above the ordinary.

A friend of mine, Simon Woodroffe, perceives life as a daring adventure. Several years ago he had the idea of starting a sushi restaurant. Today one of the several branches of Yo! Sushi has the largest conveyor belt of sushi in the world and Yo! Below is the most technologically advanced bar in the world. Voted Emerging London Entrepreneur of the Year '99, Simon still sees everything he does as an exciting adventure: 'I enjoy that cheeky little bit of me that wants to blow my customers' minds by giving them titillating surprises and drop-dead good value that they could never have dreamed of.' I can hear the cynics out there saying, 'Well it's all right for them, they've got the financial security to see life as an adventure.' This is backward thinking. As you commit to seeing life as an adventure you will feel secure no matter what your financial status. Security lies within you and does not depend on how much money you have in the bank.

> **Exercise:** If you saw your life as an adventure, how would it be different?

A state of enjoyment

> Most of the time I have no fun, the rest of the time I have no fun at all. *Woody Allen*

If this sounds like your life then it's time to ring the changes. I experienced a profound shift in the first half of 1999 in relation to the importance of enjoyment. In the space of two months my grandmother on my mother's side and my grandfather on my father's side died. They had both lived full and memorable lives in their different ways. My grandmother was a leading architect in the 1930s and my grandfather had helped invent a metal at Ford Motor Company. My grandmother came from a wealthy Jewish family and lived a life of luxury. My grandfather, from a coal-mining family in the North of England, built his life up from very little. Despite their differences the main quality that they shared was the capacity for enjoyment. I shall always remember my grandfather's smiling face as he joked with the nurse the day before he died, and my grandmother who only months before her death had been dancing at the wedding of one of my cousins! Following their deaths I was left with an overwhelming sense of how precious life is and that it is our responsibility to make the most of each moment.

It is tempting to postpone enjoyment. Do you ever catch yourself telling yourself that you'll relax and enjoy yourself once you've paid the bills, cleared the in-tray, got married, got divorced, had kids, got rid of the kids, bought a house, paid off the mortgage, retired . . . ? The truth is that to enjoy yourself is a choice only you can make. When you resist enjoyment, then resentment and bitterness creep in. You feel jealous of others, believing that they are enjoying themselves more than you are, when it's only your own conditioning that prevents you from enjoying your life to the full.

Give yourself permission to enjoy yourself today. The choice to do so will benefit all areas of your life. As you continue to enjoy yourself, any resistance you experience will dissolve. Remind yourself that there is tremendous value in enjoying yourself. You are a happier person. You are more loving and tolerant. You are fun to be with.Let yourself off the hook and dare to enjoy!

> **Exercise:** Reflect on ten things you really enjoy and do one today.

A state of happiness

> There is no duty we so much underrate as the duty of being happy. By being happy we sow anonymous benefits upon the world. *Robert Louis Stevenson*

Bobby McFerrin got it right when he sang, 'Don't Worry, Be Happy'. Unfortunately we find this one of the hardest things to do. Although happiness is so natural to our Higher Self, we have learned to block it as a result of fearful thinking and false pre-requisites. Robert Holden affectionately labelled this condition 'Happychondria' – the fear of happiness. It might seem quite a bizarre idea to think that we fear happiness. Surely we all just want to be happy? Yes we do, but the learned fear of happiness can cloud our experience of it.

Some of the fearful beliefs that clients have revealed to me are: 'I can't be happy when there is so much suffering in the world.' 'If I'm happy other people will be jealous.' 'Happiness is superficial.' 'Happiness is selfish.' 'Happiness is expensive!' 'I won't want to work if I'm happy.' 'Happiness is followed by a fall.' With this type of thinking it is no wonder that we postpone happiness for a rainy day!

Studying the rationale behind these ideas dispels the myths that we have formed. The truth about happiness is that it is your gift to the world. Being happy means that you have more to give. Happiness is a selfless state because it is contagious. When you are happy, your natural inclination is to share it. For example, if you're watching a beautiful sunset you want others to enjoy it; knowing others are deriving happiness from it enhances your own experience.

The beauty of happiness is that it's free. It costs nothing to give a hug, say a kind word and pass on a little happiness. In the words of Mother Teresa, 'Let no one ever come to you without leaving better and happier. Be the living expression of God's kindness; kindness in your face, kindness in your eyes, kindness in your smile, kindness in your warm greeting.'

Being happy is a decision only you can make. As you open the door to happiness, happiness will enter. It can feel risky to be happy because you have been conditioned to believe that you need reasons to be happy. One of the primary teachings at The Happiness Project is, 'unreasonable happiness', i.e. being happy for no particular reason. As you let go of the need to justify happiness you open yourself to the experience of unconditional happiness.

Exercise: Write down five habits of a happy person. Include attitude and outlook on life, behaviour and characteristics. Reflect on how you could embody these habits.

A state of appreciation

Gratitude is the shortest shortcut to happiness. *Barry Neil Kaufman* (author of *Happiness Is A Choice*)

Happiness and appreciation go hand in hand. As you develop your capacity to appreciate you will find more and more things to appreciate. One of the most powerful exercises that we recommend at The Happiness Project is to keep a gratitude journal in which you record what you are grateful for. This has had a more positive impact than virtually any other suggestion we have offered. Invest in an attractive hardback notebook and start by writing ten things that you are grateful for each day. At first you might find this difficult, but as you continue with the journal it will become easier and you will spot more and more things. Ideally, you should keep this going for ninety days. When you repeat something for twelve weeks, it becomes ingrained in your thought patterns and responses to life.

When I awake in the morning I give thanks for another day, for the gift of being alive, for the love I receive from Veronica, for my health, for my family and for my work. By giving thanks for the challenges in my life too, I learn to make peace with them. When I reflect on the major turning points in my life I realise that they were usually laced with difficulty and pain: for example when my parents divorced, when my first major relationship ended and when past business relationships broke down. Now that these events have been resolved I experience appreciation for each one because I recognise the extraordinary lessons they taught and the growth that has occurred. Appreciation is the natural outcome of healing and resolution.

Exercise: Count your blessings. What are you truly grateful for in your life?

A state of compassion

The human heart has the extraordinary capacity to hold and transform the sorrows of life into a great stream of compassion. *Jack Kornfield* (author of *A Path With Heart*)

To live with compassion is to bring unconditional love into each situation we encounter. Obviously this is a high objective, yet by setting out each day with the intention to be compassionate, with ourselves and with those whose paths cross ours, we awaken the stream of compassion within.

One of the many gifts of compassion is that it provides a context and meaning for the pain and sorrow we experience. On the streets of New Delhi I witnessed the terrible poverty and squalid conditions that people lived in. One part of me felt helpless and insignificant in being unable to help, but I also knew that by opening my heart and allowing my compassion to arise I was fulfilling a function. Mother Teresa emphasised that when the love in our hearts is released, we are able to care for others with true joyfulness, altruism and peace; she said, 'There are no acts of greatness, simply small acts done with great love.' Extending compassion to yourself or another is the performance of a small act with great love.

Reflect on how you can bring compassion into your daily existence, thereby lighting it up with the power of love. We have been conditioned to believe that compassion is a sign of weakness and that if we are compassionate we will get walked over in this tough world. This is a mistaken belief: compassion is an expression of our true nature and an extension of our strength.

To apply compassion in a relationship means that you need to set clear limits and boundaries. This requires you to say 'no' when you mean 'no' and 'yes' when you mean 'yes'. I once worked with a person who had no boundaries; she was like a sponge absorbing everybody else's problems. In her mind she was showing compassion by spending hours of her time listening to everyone's troubles but she would end up feeling burnt out and resentful. This was not compassion but a form of sacrifice. Sacrifice occurs when you stop following your own heart and give out of fear or guilt. To let go of sacrifice raises your self-worth and also supports those around you because you are no longer playing the role of martyr.

True compassion nourishes you; it feeds your soul by connecting you to a picture bigger than your own individual life. The Dalai Lama is a living example of the power of compassion. In his book, *Ancient Wisdom, Modern World*, he writes,

'History shows that most of the positive or beneficial developments in human society have occurred as the result of care and compassion. Consider, for example, the abolition of the slave trade . . . Compassion and love are not mere luxuries. As the source both of inner and external peace, they are fundamental to the continued survival of our species.

Exercise: Commit to opening your heart to yourself and others.

A state of power

Power has become equated with negative behaviours such as control, manipulation, corruption and greed so that many people shy away from the notion of their own power. But power is what you gain when you honour your feelings and are true to yourself. The outcome of doing this is that you experience 'personal empowerment' – feeling good about yourself. When you are in your power you feel that you can handle anything. In fact you welcome challenge because you know that it contributes to your learning and development.

To focus on the emotional states described above increases your personal power. You take responsibility for your experiences, rather than blaming the world for upsets and mishaps. You see the blessing in each event and move forward with your life. You speak your own mind, rather than saying what you think you 'should' say.

When a client called Anthony began to live in his power he decided to give up drinking, change his diet, start exercising, communicate with greater honesty and be more proactive at work. It took all his strength to stay true to himself because other people expressed their fear that they were going to lose the Anthony they knew and liked, and they felt quite threatened. It seemed there was an unspoken agreement that in order not to rock the boat, he needed to stay the way he was. As he persisted with his new-found personal power he began to notice it rubbing off on others. A friend called to tell him that he was giving up smoking, another friend told him that he was giving up alcohol and members of his family turned to him for emotional support. It was a revelation for Anthony to watch the ripple effect of his new choices. Not only did he feel better about himself as he followed his truth but he also saw that he was genuinely helping others by being an example of personal power.

Being in your power helps you to let go of emotional patterns and frees you to have the happiness and peace of mind that brings you true success.

Exercise: If you were to live in your power, how would your life be different?

When One Becomes Two

By learning how to feel comfortable with difficult emotions, you can definitely improve the quality of your relationship with yourself. This, in turn, is bound to improve the quality of all your relationships – and thus your sense of ease with and enjoyment of others. The next chapter gives you the necessary insights to build on this foundation, enabling you to enjoy your relationships to the full.

3

Relationship Insights

Everyone I have ever met or worked with is either enjoying a relationship, recovering from a relationship, looking for a relationship, struggling in a relationship or taking a break from a relationship.

Whichever situation you are in, you will probably be looking for ways to improve your relationships. They are your most powerful learning ground since your doubts, insecurities and frailties, as well as your strengths, hopes and qualities, are highlighted by the very nature of your participation in a relationship. They can be the source of your deepest joy as well as your greatest pain. Developing your understanding about relationship dynamics, releasing unresolved issues and creating a clear vision for your relationships gives you the opportunity of enjoying healthy and loving relationships.

Most of us have placed our best bet for happiness on relationships. The outcome of this is that we tend to expect too much from them. We want our partner to be completely perfect in every area, physically, emotionally, mentally and spiritually. We demand that they meet our every need and if they don't, we're off searching for the next Mr or Ms Right. But it is a myth to believe that there is only one right person who will be the answer to all your needs. Certainly there are people who are more compatible than others and the romantic notion of falling in love is still valid, but once the initial infatuation subsides you are left with the reality of domestic bliss!

Relationships need to be constantly worked on if they are to be fully functioning and enjoyable. Romantic love is not sufficient to carry a relationship through all the perils of life. Both parties must take responsibility in the relationship, must commit to clear communication and seek to understand each other's deepest needs. By doing this you create the foundation for a shared vision in which you can experience unity and joining. It is as a result of this commitment that you achieve closer intimacy.

THE FIVE STAGES OF RELATIONSHIPS

An inspirational teacher with whom I studied relationships was Sondra Ray, founder of the Loving Relationships Training. In her book *Essays on Creating Sacred Relationships* she presented the following report by researchers at the Hazelton Clinic in Minnesota. After studying a cross-section of the American population they made the following observations about the typical stages of relationships and how long they last:

1. The Dream Stage (romance): lasts up to two months;
2. The Disillusionment Stage: lasts up to two years;
3. The Misery Stage: can last up to thirty years;
4. The Enlightenment Stage: when the couple finally stops blaming each other and takes responsibility;
5. The Mutual Respect Stage.

It came as something of a shock to me to realise that we have the potential to stay unhappy for so many years, until I reflected upon my own relationship history! Before getting married I had been in a succession of short-term relationships, ranging from a few hours to three years. In most of these we were able to enjoy the dream stage as long as we spent only short periods of time together. As soon as we spent extended time together we would head into the disillusionment stage, at which point there was usually a parting of the ways. Tell-tale signs of the disillusionment stage are when the unique traits that endeared you to this person become reasons to leave the relationship. For example, when they used to arrive late for your dates together you enjoyed the anticipation of the wait. When you reach the disillusionment stage you perceive yourself as too busy to be kept waiting and you interpret their lateness as a sign of incompetence and lack of caring. In the dream stage the small gifts and cards they sent you were received with gratitude, and cherished; in the disillusionment stage you interpret them as forms of pressure and manipulation – if you get any at all! Disillusionment is a result of having too high expectations of your partner. Once they fall off their perch in your mind, you lose interest and commitment wanes.

A longer-term relationship offers the potential for the misery stage. This has also been described as the 'dead zone', when there is a breakdown in communication, loss of sexual activity and intimacy and you set your partner up as your enemy. The main dynamic that exists here is the projection of unresolved issues from your past on to your current partner. You perceive them as the source of your unhappiness and frustrations, whereas it is your own lack of awareness that is the contributing factor to this stage. Symptoms of the misery stage include constant fighting and arguing, affairs, blame, complaining about your partner behind their back, and believing that you would be happier if you were on your own. If you have been in this stage for some time it is still possible to transform the relationship by taking responsibility, resolving past issues, communicating effectively and renewing your relationship values.

To be proactive in this way moves you into the enlightenment stage, which is a sign of your spiritual and emotional maturity. The relationship is no longer the dumping ground for unresolved issues and you recognise that it offers you the opportunity for healing and happiness. You work together in a creative partnership that produces far greater results than if there was just one of you. The outcome of the enlightenment stage is synergy, a state in which the whole is greater than the sum of its parts. The essence of creating synergy is to value your differences so that you can derive benefit from each other's unique qualities.

Enlightenment leads you into the stage of mutual respect, when you experience true partnership and unconditional love. This stage is characterised by the quality of authenticity, each person being genuine, which allows the relationship to be renewed moment to moment. Both individuals are freed from their fears and doubts and trust fully in the journey they share. Communication is made from a loving place as each partner recognises the divinity within the other. The final outcome of this stage is the enjoyment of peace.

It is useful to be aware of these stages because it gives you indicators of what is required when you are in them. Of course most of us would like to stay in the dream stage for ever, but since relationships are always evolving and changing it is unrealistic to expect to be on a permanent honeymoon. When you are in the dream stage it is valuable to practise mindfulness, to witness the romance and passion of the relationship while avoiding becoming overly attached to the excitement. If you do become too grasping of the romantic love then you can develop blind spots to other dynamics in the relationship. You may overlook certain communication issues or your expectations may become too high, causing the relationship to crash in the disillusionment stage.

When you find yourself in the disillusionment stage and you choose to stay in the relationship, take your partner off the pedestal where you have put them. By doing this you open the door to the development of true friendship, which is the foundation of the future relationship. Communication can become more emotionally honest and the original love that you experienced is allowed to resurface. This stage is comparable to adolescence, when you realise that your parents are not Superman and Superwoman. They have their vulnerabilities and weaknesses just like any other human being. The development of compassion is the key to using the experience of disillusionment as an opportunity to get closer.

The misery stage is a challenging time. Since it is caused by lack of awareness, it requires a great willingness to learn and grow to resolve it. Both people have slipped into 'roles', which are unconscious behaviours that create feelings of deadness and boredom. If you experience these emotions it is a wake-up call to become conscious of the roles you are playing. Maybe you are behaving in the same way as one of your parents did in their marriage, or how you think you 'should' behave. Caught in a role, you are removed from your natural joy and sense of aliveness. Unhappiness is projected on to the relationship and you blame it for your lack of fulfilment. Until you take responsibility for the creation of the roles and are willing to change, you will be in the dark about the value of the relationship. People who end a relationship at this stage often experience the same issues in their next relationship, because the cause of the problem is unresolved.

By having the courage to work through the misery stage you reach the enlightenment stage. The relationship has matured but it is important to be aware that it is still possible to slip back into old patterns. A subconscious pattern of fear or guilt may be activated which gets projected on to the relationship. The temptation can be to judge the relationship in a negative light so it is essential to take responsibility, to increase your awareness and to let go of past roles or patterns.

Thankfully the stage of mutual respect lends itself to a greater level of permanence since there has been a genuine resolution of past issues and future fears. It requires a deep commitment to ideals such as love, honesty and trust, which provide the basis for the continuing development of the relationship.

THE THREE RELATIONSHIP DYNAMICS

It is important to become aware of the dynamics that exist in the creation of a relationship, If these are not recognised they can cause you to create undesirable patterns.

You attract what is familiar

A client called Liz came to see me complaining that none of the men she attracted could ever commit. They presented a range of different excuses to her including, 'It's not the right time', 'I have too many commitments at work', 'I am still in recovery from a previous relationship', 'I don't want to be trapped' and 'I am afraid of hurting your feelings'. She felt powerless and helpless and was on the verge of giving up on relationships altogether. In each case she would try and help the man with his issue of commitment but this only seemed to make it worse.

I suggested to Liz that she take a look at her own feelings about commitment. She came from a family in which her father made continuous threats to leave her mother. Whenever there were difficult times he would leave the house and as a family they were left feeling helpless, not knowing when he was going to return. Liz realised that subconsciously she expected men to have a problem with commitment and that she attracted men who fitted her picture. She believed she wasn't worthy of attracting a man who was willing to commit because she blamed herself for her father's lack of commitment. She believed that if she had somehow been a better daughter he wouldn't have been so uncommitted. By changing her mind about herself Liz was able to recognise that she was not responsible for her father's behaviour. She could see that she was worthy of attracting a man who wanted commitment and that it was in her power to spend time only with someone who was open to this.

As your awareness of the dynamic grows you learn to make new choices that free you from repeating the same pattern. If you attract people who have problems with areas such as intimacy, sexuality, communication, work or money, then by resolving the dynamic within yourself you can attract a different type of person. If you are already in a relationship, the problem dissolves.

You project what is unresolved

The second dynamic to watch out for is that you project unresolved issues on to your current relationships. I worked with a man called Peter who revealed that he felt the women he had been with were possessive and insecure. He noticed that as soon as he interpreted their behaviour as being possessive he would feel suffocated and trapped. This caused him to withdraw and spend more time at work or with his male friends. When we applied the understanding of this dynamic, Peter realised that he had felt emotionally suffocated by his mother: she had been very loving, but he sensed that she had been unhappy in her marriage and had channelled her emotional energies into her relationship with him. As a result, as soon as a woman gave him a certain amount of love and attention it reminded him of feeling emotionally suffocated by his mother. Subconsciously he projected this feeling, and perceived his partner as possessive and insecure.

Having recognised this form of projection he learned to communicate his feelings when they next arose. He asked his partner whether she felt possessive and insecure, rather than making an assumption. He discovered that she didn't feel possessive and realised that it was his own projection. They could then make a conscious choice about taking the relationship forward while being mindful of the dynamic of projection.

You manifest what is unresolved

The third dynamic causes you to manifest what is unresolved from your past. This is illustrated by the daughter of an alcoholic father. In her subconscious mind is the belief that all men are alcoholics. The impact of this conditioning is so strong that if she attracts a man who is not an alcoholic, she will drive him to drink to prove her belief. Many of the stereotypical patterns that we observe in relationships are formed by this dynamic.

Recently I was a guest on a television programme in which the discussion was based on the stereotype, 'Men can't commit'. I was invited to give my point of view, which is that men are capable of commitment. During the programme I was surprised by the strength of conviction that certain women had that men are unable to commit. I was sensitive to the fact that they had been hurt in past relationships. But when I pointed out that by entering a relationship with that particular belief it would become a self-fulfilling prophecy, they demonstrated that they would rather hold on to it than see things differently.

Changing these dynamics takes a small amount of 'how to' and a large amount of 'want to'. Your willingness holds the key to letting go of past conditioning and embracing new possibilities.

HOW TO CREATE YOUR IDEAL RELATIONSHIP

I first met Veronica at a seminar led by Sondra Ray entitled, 'The Next Step'. I was instantly attracted to her, and since she lived in Tokyo at the time and was leaving in the next few days I invited her out. She cancelled our arrangement at the last minute and I didn't have any further contact with her. It so happened that a year later, Veronica organised a series of workshops for Sondra and Diana Roberts in Japan. They both talked to Veronica about me, and then upon returning to London they talked to me about her. A little matchmaking was going on. Within days I was thinking about her at regular intervals and then she appeared in my dreams at night. I sought her phone number and called her up. We started an expensive long-distance phone relationship that culminated when we met up in India that summer. I met her outside the very beautiful Bahai temple in New Delhi. It is built in the shape of a lotus leaf, which is symbolic of love. We sat inside the temple and observed the code of silence. It was an extra-ordinary reunion. The next few weeks were spent catching up on each other's lives. We related story after story of our relationship experiences and discussed all our fears and doubts about them.

One month later I returned to London and Veronica went back to Tokyo. We let go of the relationship since we did not know when we would meet again. We kept in close touch on the phone and that Christmas she came to London. We were still unsure about the future so we made the most of our time together and once again said a difficult farewell. Three months later we made the decision that Veronica would move to London. One year later, we celebrated our marriage. If anyone had tried to tell me before-hand the course of the events that led up to our marriage I would never have believed them. During the entire experience I learned to let go, trust and surrender to the destiny of the relationship. If I had become overly attached and tried to force it at any stage I know that it wouldn't have worked.

We would all like to create our ideal relationship. Even if you are already enjoying a successful relationship, the following three principles are useful guidelines.

Knowing what you want

Often when you ask someone what they truly want in a relation-ship, they start off by telling you what they don't want. Since most of us have had painful and difficult experiences in relation-ships we can readily say 'I don't want to be hurt', 'I don't want someone who is possessive or jealous' or 'I don't want someone who is deceitful'. It can be more challenging for us to state what we really do want. A good starting point is to make a shopping list of the qualities – mental, physical, emotional and spiritual traits – that you want in your ideal partner.

Your list might include some of the following: a loving, happy, peaceful, healthy, generous, understanding, successful, creative, humorous, relaxed and spiritual person who is honest, com-passionate, open-minded, trustworthy, a good communicator, who has a beautiful, sexy, fit and healthy body and who enjoys art, music, learning, friends, lovemaking and travel.'

Let your imagination run wild. See if you can create a clear picture in your mind's eye of how it feels to be with this person, how you communicate together, the level of intimacy and the lifestyle you share. To strengthen this image you can make a treasure map, which is a visual tool of the relationship. By cutting out pictures and words from magazines that capture what you want and pasting them on to a piece of card, you create a collage to represent your ideal relationship. Remember to put a photo-graph of yourself in the middle! The more you clarify this vision, the more likely you are to create it.

Once you have become clear about the type of person you want to be with, then you need to work on releasing any sub-conscious blocks you might have to attracting this person into your life.

Clearing the blocks

Sarah came to see me suffering from the pain of a recent separation. She told me that her last partner had been so perfect that she had had difficulty believing that the relationship was real. They had seemed to be enjoying a mutual attraction, then suddenly he pulled away and it was over. At first Sarah just needed to offload her emotional upset, but once she became stronger she could begin the journey of exploring her blocks in relationships.

We used an exercise first devised by Sondra Ray, called the 'Truth Process', which facilitates the discovery of unconscious blocks. It consists of three parts and begins by looking at the beliefs that you hold about your present situation. On a piece of paper you write, 'My beliefs about the situation are . . .' and put down the first thoughts that come into your mind. Sarah wrote, 'My beliefs about relationships are . . .'

- They never work.
- The men I love leave me.
- I can't have the relationship I want.
- They're too much like hard work.
- They are restricting.
- It's scary to be honest in a relationship.
- Intimacy is too threatening.
- Men can't handle my love.

By doing this she clearly saw how her relationship was influenced by these types of thoughts. This awareness enabled her to reverse her old beliefs and focus her thinking in a way that would support her in future relationships. Sarah's thoughts now were:

- My relationships work.
- The men I love stay with me as long as we are mutually supportive.
- I can have the relationship I want.
- Relationships are life enhancing, fun and loving.
- Relationships are a source of freedom.
- It's safe to be honest in a relationship.
- Intimacy is a wonderful adventure.
- Men can handle my love.

She worked with these new thoughts by writing them down, using a response column to let go of any resistance and reading them regularly in order to remind herself that she had another way of looking at relationships.

Next, explore any subconscious 'payoffs' or hidden benefits you get from the types of relationship you have. Sarah found this a challenging exercise because consciously she couldn't think of any payoff from her recent separation. When she started to write them down she was surprised by what she discovered. Her responses included:

- I was able to prove that my beliefs about relationships are 'right'.
- I was able to feel sorry for myself.
- I got love and attention from others.
- I could go out with my girlfriends and complain about men.
- I could focus on myself again and not worry about anyone else.

The subconscious payoffs are behaviour patterns that don't support you. By being honest about these behaviours you can let them go and make new choices for the future.

The final part of the exercise is to reflect on any fears you might have about changing your experience in relationships. Consciously you might want to have a different experience but subconsciously you may fear what might happen. Facing the fear allows you to move forward with greater confidence and certainty. Here is Sarah's list of fears:

- If I have a great relationship I might lose my friends.
- I won't have anything to complain about any more.
- People will be jealous of me.
- I don't deserve a successful relationship.
- I would have no more excuses to hold back in my life.

By admitting these fears Sarah found that she could look upon the separation in a new light. She saw the valuable lessons that she had learned from the relationship and how she could overcome the blocks to having what she wanted.

Letting go of attachment

The third step is letting go of your attachment to creating your ideal relationship. By doing this you are able to establish objectivity. You witness your relationship journey as if you were a neutral observer. This builds a reservoir of inner strength and trust, so that you are surrendered and relaxed, rather than facing relationships with desperation or neediness. No one enjoys going out with a desperate person. You are far more attractive when you're in a trusting place. You then become a magnet that attracts what you desire.

A useful way to let go is to imagine how you would feel if you had the relationship of your dreams. When I ask people to do this they say that they would feel good about themselves, relaxed, able to get on with life and fulfilled. Creating these feelings before having a relationship releases your expectations and demands. Relationships based on neediness never truly work. It is when two people are fulfilled in their own lives that true partnership is experienced.

The main quality required for letting go is infinite patience. There is a challenging line from *A Course in Miracles* that says, 'Infinite patience for immediate results'. It goes on: 'Those who are certain of the outcome can afford to wait, and without anxiety.' The development of patience helps you to remove any doubts about creating the right relationship. As your doubts dissolve you can let your true self be revealed, which is when you are at your most attractive.

FROM SURVIVING TO THRIVING RELATIONSHIPS

Your partner is not your parent!

In Sondra Ray's Loving Relationships Training, there was always a profound silence in the room when the section on parents and relationships was reached. The main insight taught was

> **Anything unresolved in your relationship
> with your parents surfaces in your
> present relationships.**

This means that until past resentments, grievances and fears are resolved, they can have a negative influence on your relationships now. If this seems like doom and gloom, the good news is that if you are experiencing difficulty in a relationship, the root cause of the problem probably lies in the past, not the present. Unless you have healed your relationship with your parents, you will see your current relationship through distorted lenses.

Your parents were your first role model of a relationship

In my relationship courses I ask participants, 'How many of you would like your relationship to be the same as your parents'?' Ninety-five per cent respond with a resounding 'No.' Common reasons include: 'They were always fighting', 'They showed very little love for each other', 'They didn't listen to each other', 'The marriage ended in divorce', 'They worried about money all the time'. With these types of scenario it is understandable that we want a different experience.

Although we hope not to copy our parents' relationship, subconsciously we have often followed in one of two main ways: either we have conformed and recreated the same dynamics that we observed in them, or we have rebelled and attempted to create the opposite. Resolving your relationship with your parents allows you to create a healthy state in your relationship now and prevents the transference of unresolved feelings, which cause problems and misunderstandings.

The following exercise, which you can either write out or do verbally, is a useful method to discover how you have created relationships similar to your parents'.

1. Three things I dislike about relating to my current or most recent partner are . . .
2. Three things I disliked about the way my parents related to each other were . . .
3. Three things I want to improve in my current relationship are . . .
4. Three things I wanted my parents to improve in their relationship were . . .

As you read over the different lists, see how many things there are in common between your relationship with your current or most recent partner, and your parents' relationship.

One client's list included the following:

1. Something I dislike about relating to my partner is that she changes her mind at the last minute whenever we are about to go out, causing us to be late.
2 Something I disliked about the way my parents related to each other was that my mother would always fuss over her clothes, the dinner and the baby-sitter whenever they were about to go out.
1. Something I dislike about relating to my partner is that she worries about money and yet continues to overspend.
2. Something I disliked about the way my parents related to each other was that my mother worried about money while my father overspent recklessly.
3. Something I want to improve in my current relationship is to communicate with more love.
4. Something I wanted my parents to improve in their relationship was to listen more to each other.
3. Something I want to improve in my current relationship is to increase the level of trust.
4. Something I wanted my parents to improve in their relationship was to be honest so that they could trust each other.

By becoming aware of the similarities he could discuss·them with his partner and they could then work together on changing these habits.

Healing disapproval

Another dynamic that can be unresolved from the past is that of disapproval. Often a parent shows disapproval of a child as a means of attempting to correct their behaviour. The child equates disapproval with being loved because it is a way to receive attention. See if you relate to the following scene:

Billy is six years old when he leaves his bicycle in the driveway at the time his father gets home from work. The first thing his father usually does upon arriving home is to pour himself a drink and to put his feet up in front of the television. Seeing the bike in the driveway causes him to go looking for Billy and scold him for leaving it in an inconvenient place. The next day Billy does the same thing. The father comes home and once again criticises him for leaving it in the driveway. Billy concludes that getting some attention from his dad is better than no attention, even if it's in the form of disapproval.

This dynamic can manifest in a relationship if one partner subconsciously looks for disapproval as a form of love. I worked with a couple in which the wife felt constantly disapproved of by her husband. She felt that he criticised everything about her – the clothes she wore, the food she cooked, the way she looked after the children and her personal interests. When we discussed it she realised that he reminded her of her father and that she was projecting these unresolved feelings on to the marriage. The husband became aware that his father had been disapproving of his mother and that subconsciously he had slipped into behaving like him. By identifying this habit they were able to commit to undoing the need to have disapproval in the marriage.

Begin to notice if you criticise your partner or if they disapprove of you. If this is the case reflect on the disapproval that you each received in your childhood and choose to approve and appreciate each other now.

Forgiveness and your parents

Willingness to forgive is a key component in resolving your relationship with your parents. The ego struggles with this concept because it would rather be right about your parents' mistakes than allow you to forgive and make peace. Forgiveness is your ability to see beyond their actions and to recognise that they were a product of their own upbringing.

A client called Barbara came to me filled with pain and grief from her childhood. She had been molested by her father and could not create healthy, functioning relationships as an adult. She constantly attracted men who only wanted a sexual relationship, leaving her feeling guilty and ashamed. It was difficult for her to embrace the idea of forgiving her father. She blamed him for her current unhappiness and yet she knew that to see him as the enemy held her back. She recognised that in order to create a healthy, loving relationship she needed to resolve the relationship with him.

Barbara started with a small amount of willingness to forgive and let go. She hit walls of resistance as the memories of what happened returned. I reminded her that whatever feelings were surfacing were there to be healed. Barbara began to feel that she was not alone when she was choosing forgiveness, as if there was a power helping her. She felt surrounded by a sense of peace while forgiving her father. Eventually she was able to think of him and experience feelings of love. As her perception of her father shifted she began to feel better about men in general. She started to attract men who genuinely wanted to get to know her and with whom she could develop a friendship. Finally, Barbara chose to meet up with her father again after many years apart. It was an emotional reunion in which she communicated the depth of feelings from the past. She was clear that she was expressing herself from a place of love, rather than wanting to blame and cause him any grief. She told him that she had forgiven him and wanted to build a friendship for the future.

Completion letters

The major tool that you can use to reach forgiveness and resolution in your relationship with your parents is to write letters. These are called 'completion letters' and in them you write down thoughts and feelings that you have not communicated from the past. Completion means to make whole. Working with these letters heals the fragments and rifts that have occurred between you and your parents. It is important to recognise that these letters are for your own personal wellbeing. Since many of us have had difficult relationships with our parents, in which we felt wronged or emotionally deprived, there can be resistance to working with these letters. But at the end of the day it is the person who carries grudges and grievances who continues to suffer.

There are three forms of completion letters. The first letter is purely for your own therapy. In it you express anger, hurt and blame that you have not communicated. For some it is a very powerful experience as memories of abuse, betrayal, guilt or fear are activated. Sharing this letter with a therapist, loving friend or partner helps to release the feelings. Do not send this letter. This is for *your* healing and once it has been reviewed you can either burn it or throw it away.

The second letter is a forgiveness letter in which you aim to let go of your past feelings and move towards acceptance. This can be difficult because you might experience resistance to forgiving a parent for past pain. Once again the key is your willingness to focus on love and let the rest go. Writing the forgiveness letter enables you to move to a balanced place, which brings you on to the third and final letter.

In this you express your honest feelings, with the intention of resolving past conflict and making peace. By taking responsibility for your experience of the relationship you are able to reveal your feelings without blaming the parent. The guideline for writing this letter is that you would feel good if you received it yourself. Ideally you send this letter to your parents. If one or both of your parents are no longer alive there is still tremendous value to be gained from writing the letters because healing occurs during the process of writing. If you do choose to send them it is important to release your attachment to the outcome and free yourself from expectations.

My personal experience of writing these letters was profound. Following the divorce of my parents, I found it difficult to enter my father's new life. Our communication was delicate and I was unsure of where to begin to heal the rift. I worked on the first two versions and then plucked up the courage to write the third and final letter. I experienced such a sense of relief that rather than waiting to post it, I phoned and arranged to see my father the next day. It was clearly a shock to his system when I sat him down and told him my feelings about the past. But it was a real sign of his love that he could hear the difficult things I had to say, and it turned out to be the beginning of a completely transformed relationship.

I had always enjoyed a close relationship with my mother but it was still challenging to send the letter, since I was afraid that it might upset her. As it turned out, she was extremely grateful for my desire to improve the relationship and it allowed our communication to become more loving and open.

Many people feel that this type of communication is too risky or threatening. It is important to be patient and compassionate with yourself as you work on the letters. I counselled a lady called Emma, who had had a troubled history with her parents. She had eventually left her country of origin to create a new life in England. She missed her family, though, and wanted to resolve the past. The major difficulty she had experienced as a child was feeling as if her parents never understood her. They only seemed interested in her academic achievements and whenever she tried to communicate her feelings they told her to keep quiet. She went on to have a successful career but struggled to create a fulfilling relationship, a difficulty she attributed to the dysfunction in her family. It took Emma several attempts to complete her letters but at last they were ready to send. When it came to the moment of posting them she felt vulnerable and afraid. I reminded her that the true value of the letters lay in the writing of them and her willingness to let the past go. She experienced a great sense of joy as she finally sent them off, signifying her commitment to embrace a new beginning.

Here are some guidelines for writing a completion letter:

Angry, blaming letter

Dear Mum/Dad,
> What I want to communicate to you is . . .
> What I felt angry about was . . .
> What I felt betrayed about was . . .
> What I felt humiliated by was . . .
> What I felt hurt about was . . .
> What I felt scared about was . . .

What I felt ashamed about was . . .
What I felt most angry about was . . .

Read this version to a therapist, supportive friend or partner. Burn or throw it away.

Forgiveness letter

Dear Mum/Dad,
What I want to communicate to you is . . .
What I am willing to forgive you for is . . .
What I am willing to see differently is . . .
What I am willing to understand is . . .
What I am willing to let go of is . . .
What I am willing to change is . . .
What I am willing to resolve is . . .

Read this version to a therapist, supportive friend or partner. Burn or throw it away.

Completion letter

Dear Mum/Dad,
The purpose of writing this letter is to resolve our relationship from the past.
My difficulties were . . .
What I understand is . . .
What I forgive is . . .
What I want is . . .
What I value is . . .
What's important is . . .
What I appreciate is . . .
What I'm grateful for is . . .
What I love about you is . . .

Check to see if you would feel good about receiving it and read it to a therapist, supportive friend or partner for feedback. Send it when you are ready.

Clearing up your present relationships

Having focused on the influence of the past we will now turn our attention to the relationship dynamics that we experience in the present.

Your partner is not your saviour!

Do you believe that a relationship will solve all your problems? Do you imagine that having your perfect partner will fill in the missing parts of your life? Are you secretly waiting for your ideal partner to show up so that you can live happily ever after? Ending the myth that a relationship is going to be the solution to your life's problems removes the unrealistic expectations and conditions that often undermine the relationship itself.

A relationship can encourage you to be fulfilled, but it cannot make you fulfilled. No relationship can match your expectations because that is not the purpose of a relationship. The real purpose of a relationship is the exchange of love. This transcends the need for it to complete your life and places the onus on you to connect with your wholeness and love.

I worked with a couple called Tony and Sally who had been together for two years. They revealed that when they met it was the relationship of their dreams. Both of them believed that they had found their soul mate. They made plans about how they were going to spend their lives together. Prior to the relationship they had both struggled to feel good about themselves, and the relationship had finally seemed to fill that gap. They felt good when they were in each other's presence but as soon as they were apart they found it difficult to get on with their lives. Their careers began to suffer and they were losing personal friendships. Very confused, they decided to try counselling to help them resolve this situation. At first they were afraid in case anything surfaced that would threaten their relationship. They feared that if they lost it then they would lose the meaning of their lives.

I helped them to understand that by seeing the relationship as the answer to their dreams, they had placed too high expectations on being together and that they were neglecting the rest of their lives. At first it was difficult for them to face this dynamic but once they had acknowledged it they could make new choices. They saw how they perceived each other as a saviour, and committed to seeing each other differently. This enabled them to reconnect with the true sense of friendship that existed in the relationship and to create balance in each area of their life.

Clearing up your past relationships

Richard and Paul are best friends. They are six years old. Several times each day while playing they fight, fall out and are no longer best friends. Tears and tantrums follow. Five minutes later they have made up and all is forgotten. As adults we lose this ability to forgive and forget and as a result we can hold on to grievances for periods of time, even for years. *A Course in Miracles* points out that there are no small upsets and that every upset is disturbing to your peace of mind. Cast your mind back over your past relationships and reflect upon the ones which are still unresolved for you. To check if a relationship is resolved think of that person: unless you feel unconditional love and clear in your communication, it is not resolved.

Restoring harmony in your past relationships can appear to be a daunting task at first. It is reassuring to know that as you commit to the process and start to resolve one at a time, it creates a ripple effect that impacts on all your relationships. To clear them up means letting go of grievances, resentments and hurts, and having a willingness to see beyond people's behaviour.

James came to see me at a time when he was finding it hard to sustain a relationship. He had become suspicious of others since he had felt let down and betrayed in the past. He was determined to heal these feelings so he committed to resolving his past relationships. The starting point was to make a list of people with whom he still had grievances. As he began writing his list the names came flooding back – previous girlfriends, friends and associates were all put down. The next step was to prioritise the list to see which of the relationships were the most important ones to clear. (To check how resolved a relationship is, grade it on a scale of 0–10. Zero stands for completely unresolved and ten stands for totally resolved.) Following that, James wrote down the communication that he would like to make after each name. He then reflected on what would be an appropriate action. With some of the people on the list, he felt that he could communicate directly, by arranging to meet, phone or write. With others he felt that it would be more appropriate to pray for resolution, practise forgiveness and choose to let go of his past feelings. Here are some examples from his list:

◆ Julie, 4. I would like to apologise for having betrayed her trust and hurt her feelings. I played her around and I have felt guilty about my behaviour ever since we separated. It's time to let her know. Arrange to meet.
◆ Karl, 2. I felt deeply upset and angry when he had an affair with my then partner. I had confided in him the difficulties I was having in the relationship and he abused my trust. Write, and follow up with a phone call.
◆ Mike, 5. Distress about how the business didn't work out. We were both committed to the growth of the company but our differences lay in the fact that he wanted security and I wanted risk. Arrange to meet.
◆ Alice, 7. Let her know how much our friendship meant to me and that I miss not seeing her now that she has become involved in an intimate relationship. Would still like to have more contact. Phone.

As James worked through the list we discussed his fears of making the communications and the possible responses he might receive. He was afraid that he'd be rejected or laughed at. In fact what happened was a pleasant surprise. The people he spoke with were genuinely pleased to hear from him. By asking them if they had anything they wanted to communicate he enabled them to let go of their grievances. By making amends James felt as if he had finally laid the ghosts from his past and that he could get on with living fully now.

The communications that you make can be as simple as saying, 'I'm sorry'. If you have feelings of regret or guilt from the past, making a genuine apology sets you free. Notice if the ego resists and tries to make out that the other person should apologise first for justice to be done. Listen to your Higher Self. It will tell you what is the right action. Maybe it is to say to someone, 'I love you' and to thank them for the difference they have made in your life. As ever, it is important to let go of your attachment to the outcome. By doing this you release yourself from the fear that binds you, allow your heart to open and experience the love available to you now.

Relationships are mirrors

> When you meet anyone, remember it is a holy encounter. As you see him, you will see yourself. As you treat him, you will treat yourself. As you think of him, you will think of yourself. Never forget this, for in him you will find yourself or lose yourself. *A Course in Miracles*

Every relationship is a reflection of how you see yourself. For example if you treat yourself well you are treated well in relationships. If you do not experience being treated well it shows you that you need to take a look and see where you are not valuing yourself. By applying this principle you take responsibility for your experience in relationships and stop blaming others if you're not getting what you want.

This represents a shift in thinking because we have been conditioned to believe that we contribute 50 per cent in a relationship. In fact a relationship is made up of both people contributing 100 per cent and it is only when we take 100 per cent responsibility that we experience the true potential of it. By becoming aware of this dynamic you perceive how your partner can become either your enemy or your ally depending on your current state of mind. Veronica has been a blessing for me in strengthening this insight. There have been times when I have felt frustrated within my own life and wanted to blame the relationship, thinking that was where the fault lay. Thankfully she has stayed strong in these moments and has not agreed with the illusion I was projecting on to the relationship. This has enabled me to look within myself and resolve the real cause of the upset.

Think of the most significant relationships in your life and see what they are reflecting back to you. If there is anything that you would like to change in one of these relationships, think of how you can change it within yourself first. One of the most important insights to remember is that you can never change anybody else. You can only change yourself. But by changing yourself, you transform your experience in relationships.

Notice if you secretly believe that your partner should be reading this book so that they can change and then the relationship will be fine. If this is the case, then read on!

Taking responsibility for your own needs

If you expect your partner to take care of your needs you will experience conflict in your relationship. It is not the function of your partner to fulfil your needs. This is an expectation that can be developed out of childhood and works in one of two ways: (1) If you had your needs met as a child, you expect your partner to meet your needs now; (2) if you didn't have your needs met as a child, the subconscious desire to have them met now can be transferred to your partner. Either way, until you take responsibility for meeting your own psychological, emotional, physical and spiritual needs, you will experience disharmony in your relationship.

In order to have your needs fulfilled, you must find out what they are. Ask your partner which needs they perceive you to have. By doing this you involve them in the process of discovering your needs in a responsible manner. I worked with a couple, Anne and Tom, who had difficulty in fulfilling their needs. When I asked them to discuss how they perceived each other's needs it was very revealing. Anne perceived Tom as needing heaps of praise and attention, which she found demanding and draining. Tom perceived Anne as needing space and time alone but rarely taking it, which he took as a sign of rejection. By taking responsibility for finding out their own needs and involving each other in this, they could support each other without feeling resentful. Tom started to give himself praise and recognition by writing down his achievements each day, while Anne scheduled in time to be alone, giving herself the space that she required.

Taking responsibility in this way, ironically, makes it easier for your partner to give you what you want.

Giving what you want to receive

Taking responsibility for getting what you want means that you give what you want to receive. In other words, if you want to receive love, be loving. If you want to receive respect, give respect. If you want to receive understanding, seek to understand. The gift of giving is that what you give comes back to you.

True giving is a recognition that what you extend to others has been within you all the time. How can you give love if the love is not already within you? To give strengthens your connection with your Higher Self. Since the Higher Self is abundant by nature, it perceives giving as a mutually beneficial process. The ego on the other hand perceives giving as a form of loss. Since it is based on scarcity it believes that in order to give, you must lose something of value.

The willingness to give is the best way to transcend the ego. In my marriage when I have experienced a 'lack attack', and have been tempted to withhold love, understanding, money or time, the decision to give these things anyway has moved me through doubts and fears.

Think of what you want to receive in your life and give that to your partner or whoever crosses your path. Extend youself by giving that extra bit more and notice the joy that you receive by giving generously.

Learning to be a good receiver

You receive as much love in a relationship as you can handle. As soon as you are given love that exceeds your comfort threshold you will block it, avoid it or push it away. This threshold is determined by how much love you believe you deserve. The ego will convince you that you are undeserving of love and that you should sabotage the love that you do receive. The Higher Self knows that you *are* worthy of receiving the love you desire. As you place your attention on the spiritual dimension of yourself you expand your comfort zone for receiving love.

It is crucial to become a good receiver otherwise the giver can feel hurt and rejected. By discussing this dynamic with your partner you move to a place of understanding. Usually one person in the relationship is the dominant giver and the other is the dominant receiver. To bring this into balance requires both parties to be willing to change their positions. If you have been the dominant giver and your sense of identity is established through giving, then it is time to focus on receiving. Allow your partner to give to you. If you have been the dominant receiver, make the decision to give more.

One of the most difficult things for people to receive is compliments. How do you respond when someone pays you a compliment? If someone compliments you on your dress sense or hairstyle does your cynical side come forth and wonder what the hidden agenda is? Or do you genuinely say thank you and enjoy the appreciation? If someone compliments you on the dinner you served, can you just receive it or do you focus on the one dish that wasn't quite up to your standards and deflect the appreciation? The next time you are paid a compliment learn to receive it by saying 'Thank you'.

Being willing to ask for help

We all have a deep human need to feel useful and involved. Asking for help gives others the opportunity to contribute and make a difference. Usually the major block to asking for help is pride. This is a weapon of the ego that prevents you from moving forward. You stay 'stuck' in confusion or fear when asking for help would release the block.

It can be a big step to ask for help in a relationship, since this is usually associated with vulnerability. There can be resistance to letting go of defences and allowing a partner to become closer. The truth is that asking for help is a sign of strength rather than weakness: it is an act of courage to reach out and let someone in. As you do so you experience a greater level of intimacy, which dissolves your fears and doubts.

Putting yourself in your partner's shoes

One of the major sources of conflict in our marriage has been the issue of which country to live in. We have lived in England since being together and Veronica has naturally wanted to discuss the option of moving to New Zealand or Australia to be nearer her family. When the subject was raised I would get cold feet, as the idea of moving appeared threatening to me. I would attempt to change the conversation, which caused upset and distress. When we discussed this conflict it transpired that the real issue was not which country we were to live in, but my inability to put myself in her shoes and fully understand her experience. When I did project myself into her reality, Veronica felt understood and emotionally met. Seeking to understand how it felt for her to live in a country away from her family and friends provided the bridge between our different perspectives.

To put yourself in your partner's shoes requires listening with empathy, compassion and acceptance. It means setting to one side your own desire to be understood. You have to resist the temptation to jump in with your own opinion and learn to give your full attention to their point of view. Listening with empathy means that you go beyond hearing the words and you focus on discovering the meaning behind them. The challenge of this type of listening is that it is not based on logic or reason. Trying to understand your partner on a rational level is insufficient. You have to connect with them emotionally, which requires you to suspend your judgement and interpretation of what you *think* they are saying in order to hear what they really are saying.

It takes practice and patience to develop this depth of communication. Willingness to go beyond any preconditioned concepts is the key to understanding your partner. You might think you know who they are, but until you put yourself in their shoes over and over again, you will only be scratching the surface. This is how a relationship can develop to the stage of mutual respect. Your desire to know who your partner really is, rather than who you think they are, is the greatest gift you can give.

The art of listening

Truly listening is an art that requires an open mind and keen ears. We build up so many of our own beliefs and opinions that they often cloud our ability to listen objectively. We either pay lip service by pretending to listen when really we are caught in our own thinking, or we listen parrot fashion, responding without having really heard what was said. In my workshops when I ask participants what contributes to a successful relationship, the majority of responses highlight the importance of being heard and understood as an absolute priority. Our capacity to listen builds trust and intimacy and involves a commitment to avoid jumping to conclusions, making snap decisions and anticipating what you think you're going to hear.

To develop your listening skills, start by learning to listen to yourself. Notice if you get so caught up in a busy lifestyle that you fail to tune into your own needs. By taking some stillness each day you become more practised at listening to yourself. Listen to the thoughts in your mind, the feelings in your body and the calling of your spirit. As you focus more on yourself, you will have less need to assert your opinion in a relationship and have a greater capacity to listen to your partner.

You must then be willing to make listening time in your relationship. This is when each of you has the opportunity to be listened to without diagnosis, interpretation or advice. At first you might need to ask for this form of support since it can be tempting when arriving home at the end of a day to put the television on, to get distracted and to avoid creating time. As an understanding grows, the commitment to listen and to be listened to enhances the relationship.

It is particularly important to have sufficient 'air time' before going to bed each day. Sleeping on thoughts and feelings that haven't had a chance to be heard can lead to problems later on. Agree that each person in the relationship has 5–10 minutes in which to communicate what they would like to express, while their partner listens unconditionally. This means that even when there are difficult feelings to communicate, you are listened to with empathy and understanding. It enables feelings to move in a constructive way, rather than building up to be used destructively at a later date.

The art of listening requires that you do not take personally what your partner is expressing. If you do take it personally, your emotions colour your perception and you will not be able to listen compassionately. You will try and defend your position, which causes further conflict and defeats the purpose of the communication. A useful lesson from *A Course in Miracles* that can be applied to this dynamic is, 'I am never upset for the reason I think'. This means that most of the time you are seeing only the past, that you are not seeing things clearly as they are now. When your partner is expressing an upset it is probably a reaction to an old conflict, which gets projected on to their current reality. By listening with the intent to understand, you provide the opportunity for this old upset to be resolved. All upsets can be turned into set-ups for greater healing and love if there is the willingness to listen, understand and move on.

I once worked with a couple who had been married for twelve years. Their relationship had become so unhappy that the wife had asked for a divorce. They were constantly arguing and both felt misunderstood, unloved and undervalued. We sat down together to see if there was any way of resolving the differences that had arisen. We set clear boundaries about how they were going to communicate. They agreed to listen with the intent to understand and to give each other the necessary space to disclose their feelings without an initial comeback. This gave them a sense of safety and support so that they could open up to each other.

It transpired that the husband felt unappreciated. He claimed that he had put his wife's needs first by providing for her financially, supporting her career moves and not interfering with the children. The wife felt that although he provided for her in monetary terms, he never gave her what she truly wanted, which was to be loved, cherished and nurtured emotionally. She provided a home, brought up the children, cooked meals and felt that this was undervalued. She felt that she was always doing something wrong and could never please him. He felt that too many expectations were made of him. He worked long hours, travelled a lot and just wanted to come home and relax. He felt that her demands were unreasonable and that there was too much pressure on him to behave in a certain way.

Creating the space for these feelings to be shared, listening carefully to each other and being willing to see their situation differently, opened the door to change. By continuing to communicate in this manner, the couple discovered the similarity between what they were experiencing and their own past family experiences. The wife realised that her mother had felt like this in her marriage. Her father had provided on a material level but her mother had always complained that he never gave her the love she really wanted. The husband saw how his father had worked all hours, coming home exhausted and expecting to be taken care of without thinking of his wife's needs.

The clearer the scenario became, the more this couple could make new choices about their relationship. Frustration was gradually replaced by a sense of compassion and they began to feel as if they were growing together in the right direction.

Express yourself

What you don't communicate runs you on a subconscious level. The period between the time you feel you want to communicate and the time when you make the communication, is the period in which you can experience 'deadness' and the desire to leave a relationship. It is fundamental to your wellbeing that you communicate your thoughts and feelings. The greatest problems that I have witnessed in relationships and the greatest cause of relationship breakdowns stem from lack of communication.

I believe that the majority of our communication difficulties originate in our childhood. Often as children we were not encouraged to express our thoughts and feelings. In fact it was quite the opposite as we were fed messages such as, 'Children should be seen and not heard', 'Don't talk back to me', 'You shouldn't feel that way', 'How can you say that after everything I've done for you?'. Subconsciously we decide that to express ourselves can lead to undesirable consequences. We might also witness our parents arguing and fighting, which adds to our misgivings about the value of communication.

Until we resolve our negative beliefs about self-expression we will perceive it in a negative light. I had a client called Alan who had lost his confidence to express himself as a result of childhood experiences. He was a slow learner at school, for which he was teased and told that he was stupid. He developed a stammer, which his mother used to criticise. As an adult he found it difficult to connect with others and enter into conversations. He felt isolated and cut himself off from people. In our work together he was able to practise expressing himself. He discovered that he had a lot he wanted to say and that communicating it relieved him of the anxieties he carried. We set small goals for Alan: to start initiating conversations and to include himself in social situations. This developed his confidence, which led him to actively seek out opportunities to express himself.

To clarify your perception of communication, write down your beliefs about it. A collection of common beliefs include:

◆ I'm not worth listening to.
◆ You have to be careful what you say.
◆ Don't say too much otherwise it might be used against you.
◆ Communicating is challenging, but worth it.
◆ People aren't going to want to hear what I have to say.
◆ Nobody ever listens to me so why bother to express myself?
◆ Expressing myself sets me free.
◆ I might expose my vulnerability if I say what I think.

By identifying unhelpful beliefs, you can develop new thoughts that support and empower you. It then takes practice and courage to improve your communication skills. When I first started to express myself more I feared that I would end up in one conflict after another, since I associated communication with confrontation. I did experience discomfort as I became more honest and direct in my communications. But since my intention was always to be clear and loving, people valued my greater openness.

The two major fears that I repeatedly hear from clients are of hurting others and of being rejected if they express their feelings. Some examples: a forty-year-old woman who wanted to communicate her distress to her father, but was terrified that he would get upset; a married woman who wanted to tell her husband that she didn't feel understood, but was afraid that he would end the marriage, and a single man who wanted to communicate with women he is attracted to, but was afraid of ridicule. These are all potentially difficult communications but the longer the feelings are unexpressed, the greater the problem becomes.

By expressing yourself you are being emotionally honest, which may cause short-term pain as uncomfortable feelings are communicated, but you will reap the benefits of healthy self-expression. Emotional honesty allows a relationship to develop and grow. I once worked with a couple who were engaged to be married. They had a seemingly great relationship on the outside but underneath many things were unexpressed. They both had fears about the future of the relationship, which neither of them felt they could reveal to the other. Eventually they summoned the courage to express what was really going on for each of them. By doing this they were able to reconcile their differences and enter into the marriage with greater trust and honesty.

Another common dynamic is the use of third-hand communication. This is when you talk about your relationship difficulties with everyone else but the person concerned. Obviously it can be helpful if you are experiencing problems to receive support from a friend or neutral party. But if you use this as a substitute for direct communication an unhealthy backlog can develop. Having the courage to express yourself to your partner sustains and develops the relationship. It is always sad when the person whom you are supposed to love and share your thoughts and feelings with becomes the person with whom you are most afraid to communicate.

There are two main steps to follow for successful self-expression.

Taking responsibility
It is of vital importance to own what you want to say, or blame can enter the communication. Whatever has happened in the past, you are expressing your interpretation of events. One of the

most effective ways to take responsibility is to write down what you want to say before you say it. By doing this you become aware of how you may sound. If there is a strong tone of anger or blame, it provides you with the space to clear those initial feelings. It is also useful to role-play a communication to a supportive friend or in a therapeutic session to get feedback about how you come across. By beginning your communication with the words, 'In the situation involving . . . I felt . . .' it is possible to express feelings of anger, fear and hurt without blame. By saying, 'In the situation involving . . . you made me feel . . .' you are making your partner the culprit, and conflict will occur.

Communicating with the intention to create mutual understanding

If you have difficult feelings that you wish to express, having the intention to achieve love and understanding allows the communication to bring you closer rather than causing a rift. For example in my marriage if I express grievances with the intention of love and understanding then what I communicate is received openly. If on the other hand I express grievances with the intent to make Veronica feel bad or guilty then naturally the communication causes greater conflict. By getting behind the words you say, you discover the true intent of your expression.

Be willing to see things differently. Your willingness to see beyond your perception and experience of events means that your self-expression is laced with humility and a sense of surrender. This also gives your partner the opportunity to express their feelings in an atmosphere of love and understanding. If your opinion becomes fixed and rigid it causes a breakdown of communication. This defeats the purpose of expressing yourself and gives rise to misgivings about the value of self-expression.

Communication enhances your sex life!

A great benefit to be enjoyed as an outcome of successful communication is that it enhances your sex life! When we withhold communication sexual blocks are created, a deeper level of trust and intimacy is established when we communicate. The failure to express feelings such as anger, hurt or resentment can create the sensation of sexual deadness towards our partner. A relationship might be able to survive these repressed emotions in the short term but over a period of time they build up until sexual relations break down.

When you start to focus on improving your sex life you need to take into consideration the following three factors:

1. If sex was considered a taboo subject in your family then you probably grew up with the belief that it was not acceptable to talk about it.
2. If you experienced religious conditioning about sex being sinful it may have led to feelings of guilt and shame.
3. If your sex education was delivered in an atmosphere of embarrassment, this will have contributed to a sense of discomfort regarding sex and communication.

It is important to free yourself from past conditioned beliefs in order to feel comfortable talking about sex within your relationship. Start by discussing with your partner your perception of your parents' sex life. By doing this you can discover if you are carrying any of the beliefs or patterns from your parents' relationship. Steve and Kim had been experiencing sexual difficulties so they agreed to talk about their family experience. As Steve started to recall his early childhood he could picture his parents locking their bedroom door on a Friday night. His presence was not welcome. He had internalised this memory and believed that he was unwanted sexually. As a result he withheld his sexual feelings, since he feared that he would be rejected. Kim's parents had been open about sex so she felt comfortable talking about sex and interpreted Steve's withdrawn sexual behaviour as a sign that he was not attracted to her. Talking about these dynamics enabled them to clear their misunderstandings and grow closer.

Discussing your sexual history with your partner is another key aspect to creating a healthy sex life. You may have a range of emotions related to your past, which can prevent you from being fully present in your current relationship. This doesn't mean that you have to go into every detail, but be willing to talk about general patterns that you notice from your past.

One common pattern is being attracted to someone who is unavailable physically, emotionally or psychologically. This might mean being attracted to someone who is currently in a relationship, is dominated by their work or a hobby, lives in a foreign country or is recovering from a previous relationship. Other patterns include withholding sexually if you're feeling hurt or upset, not communicating what you want sexually, or frequently feeling tired and losing interest in sex. By becoming conscious of these patterns you can notice if they start surfacing in your current relationship and take action to change them.

Talking about your sexual history also helps to clear away sexual fantasies and comparisons. These draw you away from being intimate with your partner. It is common to have sexual fantasies either while you're making love or at other times. Being able to talk about your fantasies to your partner, with the intention of creating love and understanding, removes the secrecy from them, which is often the attraction of a fantasy in the first place. Comparing your partner to previous lovers keeps you 'stuck' in the past. Having the courage to communicate about making comparisons liberates you from your past.

There is great value to be gained from discussing any fears you may have about sex. These might be based on past experience or insecurities. By listening with love and acceptance to your partner when they are disclosing their fears, you increase the level of safety and trust within the relationship.

Finally, take responsibility for your sex life by discovering what your partner likes sexually, by finding out how you could improve as a lover and by letting them know how it is for you. I recommend that you choose a time when there are no other distractions and when you can commit to listening to each other in a relaxed and intimate way.

Commitment sets you free

Commitment is the choice to give yourself fully in a relationship. Unfortunately the very idea of it often fills people with fear. It is a mistake to believe that commitment ties you down, and is laden with unwelcome responsibility and obligation. By sitting on the fence and being non-committal you prevent yourself from realising the full potential of a relationship. Commitment sets you free, as it liberates you from your fears.

Until you commit you do not know the truth about a relationship. You will only experience the shadow because fear takes you away from the light. Choosing to commit does not mean that you have to get married. Even if you are together for a short period of time, being committed means that you make the most of it for the time that you are together. Commitment within a relationship provides a great sense of safety. Since it is an act of love, you have a context in which to move away from the fear generated by the ego. When you experience difficulties such as arguments, disagreements and win/lose situations, your commitment gives you the opportunity to work things out. It is a declaration of your intent that the wellbeing of each person is more important than the outcome of disputes.

Building a vision together

The vision that you have together becomes the compass that guides you towards what you want. The greater the clarity of the vision, the more likely it is that you will create it. The process of clarifying a vision within a relationship consists of discovering what is truly important for both of you, prioritising these values and creating a vision statement. A vision grows out of your commitment to be together and includes all the different components of life including your family, work, play, environment and spirituality.

Once you clarify your vision you can use it to check the health of the relationship. If you are experiencing a difficult time then you can to come back to it and see where you are off-track. This shifts your focus away from the temptation to blame one person for the state of the relationship and means that you both take responsibility for getting it back on course.

It takes focus and an open mind to work on creating a vision together. Again, schedule in some quiet time when you know that you're not going to be disturbed. The first step is for each of you to write a list of the things that you truly value in life. Your list might include some of the following:

love, enjoyment, family, peace, happiness, security, learning, people, health, integrity, success, relaxation, play, wealth, service

Now go back over the list and mark your ten main ones, prioritising these values 1 to 10. Once you have completed this, share your lists. A helpful guideline is simply to listen to each other without comment as each of you discloses your values. It is deeply rewarding to find out what is most important for your partner. It might reveal some surprises when you discover differences.

One couple who did this exercise discovered that the man's main value was adventure, whilst the woman's was security. This explained why they were often at loggerheads and enabled them to work together to agree what was important for the relationship as a whole.

Having found your personal values you can now work on creating the core values of the relationship. Bring your two lists together and choose ten of the values that you want as the foundation of the relationship. Once you have these core values in place you can discuss what needs to happen in the relationship so that you can live by them. For example if the main value is love, then you might decide:

◆ We need to have open and clear communication.
◆ We need to respect and value each other's differences.
◆ We need to be playful and have spontaneous fun.
◆ We need to accept each other and commit to forgiveness and compassion.

If the main value is security then the criteria could be:

◆ We need to be honest and respectful with each other at all times.

◆ We need to have absolute integrity in our relationships and dealings.
◆ We need to create financial independence.
◆ We need to have time scheduled together that is sacred.

These are the stepping stones to developing a vision statement together that encapsulates both your values and your needs. An example of a vision statement is:

> We have a loving, peaceful, respectful relationship, which has integrity, compassion and enjoyment at its heart. We commit to communicating with understanding, forgiveness and acceptance in order to give security and happiness. We appreciate one another and value each other's differences.

Once you have your vision statement, commit to reading it at least once a week so that it becomes integrated within the relationship. It may change over time as you continue to learn and grow together. By focusing on the vision you share a common purpose, which gives the relationship great strength and a sense of your connection.

Having created your vision you must then pull back from it, which gives the relationship breathing space and enables you to enjoy the journey of being together straight away rather than waiting until you have achieved the perfect scenario.

Setting the intention

Your vision statement sets the bigger picture for the relationship, which may take you five to ten years into the future. As you pull back from it, it is valuable to decide what is most important for your partnership each day. When you wake up in the morning, before you get into the busyness of the day, ask each other, 'What is our intention for today? What do we commit to and what is most important for us?'

This steers you both forward in the same direction and gives you a greater focus than just your daily 'to do' list. It provides a strong reference point for decision making and for guiding your actions. For example if you set the intention for love as the priority, then when you meet challenges during the day, by checking them against this intention you determine the course of action that you will take. Supposing that you are asked to work late, and you had arranged to have dinner with your partner, checking against the intention for the day guides you to answer. Defining your intention means that you are being proactive rather than merely reacting to the world around you. It adds another dimension to the relationship, lifting you out of the day-to-day routine and keeping you on track.

Being on purpose

People often ask the question, 'What is the purpose of our relationship?' By following a vision statement or setting a daily intention you are choosing a purpose in the relationship rather than waiting for it to find you.

The signposts that show you are on purpose in a relationship are feelings of peace and serenity, a deep level of trust and surrender, and the experience of joy and happiness. You can tell that you are off purpose when you experience constant conflict, power struggles, control games and competition. Being off purpose is the ego's way of trying to control the relationship. Since its motto is, 'Seek, but do not find', it encourages you to look for the purpose outside the relationship rather than turning inwards and choosing it together.

Some of the common purposes that the ego gives to a relationship are these:

- ◆ *It's us versus them.* The relationship becomes a weapon and a form of defence against the world.
- ◆ *To rescue each other.* This stems from the belief that the love we need must come from someone else, and that there's only one special person who can provide it.
- ◆ *To share desperation.* This is based on a victim mentality where the relationship feeds a negative and cynical outlook on the world.

◆ *To get rather than to give.* This is where the relationship's credo is 'What can we get?' and 'What's in it for us?'

Allowing a relationship to be run by the ego guarantees lack, disillusionment and unhappiness. The only possible outcome of an ego-driven relationship is fear. There is no trust, there is no understanding and ultimately there is no love.

To shift a relationship from the ego to spirit is to dedicate it to love. The focus becomes 'What can we give?' and 'How can we contribute?' Your goal is to see how you can make a difference in the lives of others rather than just focusing on your own personal gain.

THE PRINCIPLE OF LOVE

Implementing the following principles in addition to what you have discovered so far also helps create truly happy relationships. Sondra Ray's guiding principle about love and relationships states: 'Love brings up anything unlike itself for the purpose of healing and release.' In other words, any difficult thoughts and feelings come to the surface, giving you the opportunity to resolve them.

Picture a glass with mud in the bottom of it. If you pour water into the glass it stirs up the mud to create a murky liquid. If you continue to pour in water, the mud overflows and you are left with a clear glass. The glass represents a relationship, the water is love and the mud is anything unlike love. Pouring love into a relationship flushes out any subconscious resistance to the experience of love.

This resistance includes behaviour such as:

◆ pushing your partner away;
◆ putting your partner down;
◆ not communicating directly;
◆ being disloyal by having affairs;
◆ putting work first;
◆ focusing on personality traits that annoy you;

- wanting to leave the relationship without giving it a true chance;
- wanting to be right rather than happy;
- having more passion for a hobby, such as shopping or sport, than for the relationship;
- watching television rather than being intimate.

Identifying this dynamic allows your relationships to be your greatest teachers. They constantly offer you lessons that aid your personal growth, helping you to find greater peace and happiness. I worked with a client called Tony who had just entered a new relationship. His previous relationship history had been dominated by dysfunctional and destructive patterns. This new relationship was completely different from anything he had experienced before. He felt loved and accepted unconditionally, and he found that he couldn't handle it. He felt suffocated and trapped, and believed that he had to get out of it to survive. Although he really wanted to be in it, he kept withdrawing his love and removing himself. By understanding this principle, Tony saw that the relationship was a healing experience and became willing to let go of his resistance to the love that he did receive.

It is ironic that we yearn to be loved, and yet when we are loved we often feel threatened and afraid. By staying and committing to a relationship, we let the love heal whatever is unresolved within us. We come to understand that healing is part of the purpose of our being together.

A good starting point in opening yourself to love is to clear your misconceptions and negative beliefs. There are many confusing messages about love in the world, so it is vital to develop a loving relationship with love itself. See whether you relate to any of the following limiting beliefs:

- Love hurts.
- Love is cruel.
- Love is manipulative.
- Love is all-consuming.
- Love is painful.

- There is not enough love to go round.
- Love leads to heartbreak.
- It's not safe to love because it will be taken away.
- I can't get enough love.
- I don't deserve the love I desire.
- Love is expensive!

Through holding on to these types of limiting beliefs, you will either prevent yourself from experiencing love or you will sabotage the love that you do receive. The bottom line on love is that it is innocent. Love has never done anything to hurt anyone, it is not limited in any shape or form and the true effects of love are healing and happiness.

As you begin to unravel your relationship with it you look for love in different ways. You realise that the ego blocks your awareness of love's presence in your life. The process of letting go opens you to the love that comes towards you all the time. It is the fear of receiving it that prevents you from enjoying it to the full. Some helpful beliefs to focus on include:

- Love heals.
- Love is innocent.
- Love sets you free.
- Love knows no limits.
- Love is an expression of joy.
- There is an abundance of love to go round.
- Love begets love.
- It's safe to love because the more you love the more it comes back to you.
- I am available to receive love.
- I am worthy of receiving the love I desire.

In order to experience true love in a relationship, you have to be willing to let go of the idea of romantic love. Romantic love is the ego's belief that some forms of love are more special than others. *A Course in Miracles* states:

There are no different categories of love. There isn't one

kind of love between a mother and a child, another between lovers, and another between friends. The love that is real is the love that lies at the heart of all relationships. That is the love of God and it doesn't change with form or circumstance.

By looking for romantic love you get caught in the myth of the soul mate. The belief that there is a Mr or Ms Right out there is an illusion. When you are obsessed with looking for your soul mate you close yourself to the potential of the relationships around you. Even when you are in a monogamous relationship there is tremendous healing and joy to be gained by opening to others.

As you open yourself to love you heal your blocks to it. This allows you to enjoy it and let go of your fear of losing it. You cannot lose love because you cannot own it in the first place. You can only surrender to it, which requires faith and courage. The act of surrendering to love connects you with your Higher Self since your Higher Self is love. When two people are connected with their Higher Selves in a relationship they experience the trust, peace, joy and happiness that are rightly theirs. Love is the gateway to everything that you want.

THE PRINCIPLE OF FORGIVENESS

Forgiveness is the application of unconditional love within a relationship. When you forgive you are choosing to see your partner through the eyes of love rather than fear. It is the choice to see the wholeness in another rather than seeing them as their limited ego self. All forgiveness is a form of self-forgiveness: as you extend forgiveness to another, you forgive yourself. Forgiving others is a sign of your willingness to give up the judgements that block you from receiving the love that you desire.

All judgement stems from the ego's desire to find fault in others, which we mistakenly believe will make us feel better about ourselves. The fact is that when we judge another we are judging ourselves. When we condemn another we are condemning ourselves. By giving up judgement we free ourselves from this self-inflicted cycle of pain.

If judgement is the crucifixion of a relationship, then forgiveness is the resurrection. To live in judgement is to feed on conflict, separation and resentment – the cornerstone of the ego. Resentment is taking poison yourself and hoping that someone else suffers. Ultimately to hold on to resentment only hurts yourself.

When someone has behaved unlovingly towards us, if they have lied, betrayed or hurt us, they have lost touch with their essence. *A Course in Miracles* tells us that everything a person does is either 'love, or a call for love'. All unloving behaviour is a call for love and is an unconscious attempt to reach out for help. If you can extend beyond your desire for blame and revenge you will be able to offer that help. To judge a person simply matches your behaviour with theirs, which keeps you trapped on the level of the ego. Forgiving someone doesn't mean that you don't point out the mistakes that they have made, but it does mean that you are willing to see the essence, love and perfection of them, which brings you the peace of mind that you seek.

Sometimes people think that to forgive in a relationship is an open door to being used and abused. This is absolutely untrue. Choosing to forgive does not mean that hurtful or damaging behaviour in a relationship is acceptable. Abuse in a relationship is a clear call for love, and that starts by loving yourself. To fully love yourself means that you do not let anyone abuse you. You walk away or do whatever you have to do to end the abusive behaviour.

I had a client called Fiona who had been in a relationship for over five years. In that time she stumbled across evidence that showed her partner was having an affair. She was devastated and confronted him with this information. At first he denied it but then had to admit to it when she revealed the evidence. Fiona was determined to leave the relationship but her partner promised that he would go into therapy, work out his problems and commit more deeply to the relationship. Fiona agreed to stay under these conditions. Shortly afterwards, during an argument about the affair, he slapped her. After the initial shock and anger had subsided she felt that she should forgive him and take him back. She thought that maybe she had provoked the fight and that it was her fault. Subconscious feelings of guilt were causing her to blame herself and feel that if only she had been more loving, caring and conscious then none of this would have happened.

When Fiona came to discuss the relationship with me I encouraged her to imagine that a friend had come to her in the same situation. This enabled her to disengage from her emotional state and see that her partner's behaviour had been abusive and damaging. We talked about the function of forgiveness and she saw that to forgive him did not mean that she had to stay with him. In fact she realised that the most loving thing to do was to end the relationship. Forgiving him meant that she didn't blame him or carry feelings of resentment and revenge. Fiona saw that ultimately this would only hurt her by keeping her hooked into the relationship. By forgiving him she forgave herself for being in the situation, and she was able to end the relationship with a sense of resolution.

This illustrates our tendency to blame ourselves if we experience abusive behaviour within a relationship. We feel ashamed, which causes us to keep the experience to ourselves. This shame is based on judgements that we carry about ourselves and that cause us to feel guilty. We believe that we deserve to be abused since we perceive ourselves as bad and wrong and deserving of punishment. Forgiveness heals the shame that binds us. We no longer project our feelings of low self-worth on to a relationship, so we no longer attract abuse.

Julie came to me with a moving story. She had just ended an eighteen-year marriage in which she had been emotionally and physically abused. It had reached the stage where she feared for her life in some of the fights. She developed cancer three years before ending the marriage, which she felt was a reflection of the anger and grief that she had contained. When she informed her husband that she wanted to separate he threatened to commit suicide. He tried to ruin her reputation in the local community and with family and friends by spreading rumours and writing spiteful letters.

Julie had many reasons to be resentful and unforgiving, but she knew in her heart that the only way forward was through forgiveness. Through forgiving her husband she felt that she could release herself from the guilt she carried. She had always believed that she was not good enough and deserved to suffer. She had played the role of the saviour in the marriage, in her family and in the community. People came to her to solve their problems and she had lost her own sense of self. As she began to rediscover her identity she could no longer fulfil these roles. As Julie forgave herself and her husband, he stopped attacking her. She made a successful recovery from her cancer and continues to work on forgiveness on a daily basis.

If you have experienced conflict in a relationship, the following five steps are guidelines for bringing yourself to a place of true forgiveness:

Choosing to forgive yourself

At first this idea can appear misleading because if you feel wronged then why should you have to forgive yourself? Forgiving yourself brings you a sense of inner peace. In this state your perception of conflict is transformed and leads to resolution.

Choosing to forgive the other person

Willingness to forgive is a decision to focus on love and let the rest go. It is natural to resist this idea because the ego would rather be right about its judgement of another than let you be happy. When you make the choice to forgive you connect with your Higher Self, which sees only love. You are able to let go of grievances and hurt because you understand the role that they have played in your healing.

Communicating with the intention of understanding and being compassionate

This is the step that makes your forgiveness real. By communicating with the intention of understanding another's position, rather than wanting to express your own opinion first, you open the relationship to the possibility of reconciliation and the restoration of harmony. This requires that you go beyond the story they give you, putting yourself in their shoes and extending compassion and acceptance.

Letting go of your attachment to the outcome

When you choose to forgive someone you may never reach the outcome that you hope for. You may feel that it is right for them to apologise, to admit their wrongdoing and to seek to make amends. You have to accept that they may never be able to take responsibility and see their mistakes. You cannot change anyone else; you can only change your mind about that person and by doing so set yourself free. Each individual has their own journey in life and you cannot tamper with this. In fact the more that you do, the greater the possibility for conflict. Your responsibility lies in your willingness to see the truth about them. By following your conscience you will know whether you have genuinely let go or not.

Peace is restored in the relationship

When true forgiveness has occurred, peace returns to the relationship. There is no problem that forgiveness cannot solve. Forgiveness is the master eraser, wiping out the past and creating a clean slate for the future. As you choose to forgive, you let go of all claim to punishment, sacrifice and suffering. Forgiveness unblocks whatever has stood between you and your highest good. As *A Course in Miracles* says, 'The holiest of all the spots on earth is where an ancient hatred has become a present love.'

THE EGO DIMENSION

The ego has a field day when it is projected on to relationships, because they are like magnifying glasses causing any fearful thoughts to loom large and clear. The ego has the same effect on relationships as it does on the relationship that you have with yourself. By projecting fear it distorts the truth about the relationship. It is useful to recognise the four primary impacts of the ego so that you can exercise compassion and wisdom when they surface in a relationship.

Judgement

The ego is the fault-finder that looks for the failings in a relationship. The dynamic of judgement drives the four core negative beliefs that you can have about yourself and projects them on to your relationship. If your core belief is 'I'm not good enough', your primary judgement of a relationship is that it is not good enough or that you are not good enough for it. By holding on to this judgement you never discover the beauty of the relationship.

If your core negative belief is 'There's something wrong with me', you will perceive your partner as not being the 'right' one and you will interpret difficulties as proof that there is something wrong with the relationship. This may cause you to want to leave the relationship until you change your mind about yourself.

If your core negative belief is 'I'm not worthy', you either see yourself as not being worthy of a relationship or think that no one else is worthy of you.

If your core negative belief is 'I'm a failure', you can either view a relationship as a failure or yourself as a failure in relationships. You block yourself from enjoying success in a relationship because it does not fit with your self-image.

Attack

The ego attacks a relationship by projecting unloving, vengeful and condemning thoughts on to it. This is the ego's form of protection. It mistakenly believes that by attacking another it is defending itself. The trouble is that all attack is a form of self-attack. *A Course in Miracles* offers the lesson, 'I can escape from the world I see by giving up attack thoughts.'

Doubt

The effects of doubt within a relationship are worry, insecurity and uncertainty. Being caught in doubt limits a relationship because you never give it a chance. It is like driving a car with your foot on the accelerator and the brake at the same time. Letting go of doubt means taking your foot off the brake so that you can move forward with ease.

Sabotage

The chief weapon of the ego is sabotage. A loving, supportive and enjoyable relationship can be too threatening for the ego to handle, so it will attempt to undermine it, creating distractions and offering seemingly more attractive options. To know that you are worthy of receiving the love in a relationship is the key to undoing the dynamic of sabotage.

By applying the same principles that we used for making the transition from the ego to the Higher Self, we can move from the ego's interpretation of a relationship to the spiritual dimension. The following steps are a gentle reminder of how to make the shift:

Set the intention: Being clear about your intention to experience both true success and happiness in relationships is the starting point for moving away from the ego.

Raising your awareness: Through having an increased level of awareness you can recognise more quickly when the ego is at work and recommit to letting it go.

Forgiveness: Practising forgiveness in a relationship is the path to peace of mind and true fulfilment. As Mark Twain said, 'Forgiveness is the fragrance the violet sheds on the heel that has crushed it.'

Acceptance: Acceptance is the practice of unconditional love. By removing the conditions you place on a relationship you open the door for miracles to occur.

Asking for help: You cannot make this journey alone. By reaching out and asking for support, whether it be from a friend, a therapist or God (as you understand God), you demonstrate your willingness and determination to experience both happiness and success in relationships.

THE SPIRITUAL DIMENSION

We tend to spend a lot of time on the mental, physical and emotional aspects of a relationship while overlooking the spiritual dimension. Focusing your awareness on the spiritual dimension balances the whole relationship. Being spiritual in a relationship doesn't mean that you are walking around in a permanent state of ecstasy! To me it simply means that within the relationship there is a commitment to love, truth, simplicity and making a difference in the world. It is a selfless way of living that turns the mindset of 'What can we get' to 'What can we give' and enables a relationship to become a vehicle for creative expression and co-operation.

Since it is a challenge to apply the ideals of spirituality and to cope with the pressures of modern life, it's important to develop ways of nurturing the spiritual dimension. One of the most powerful methods is to share silence together. This can involve the practice of meditation, going for silent walks or taking candle-lit baths in silence. Such a ritual enables you to focus on a higher vision rather than on everyday survival. Each time you connect with the spiritual dimension you strengthen the heart of a relationship.

The following five qualities are the essence of the spiritual dimension. Placing your attention on each one, you emphasise its presence in a relationship:

Love: The application of love is to be kind, respectful, accepting and forgiving. Although you probably subscribe wholeheartedly to these values it is easy to forget them when you are under pressure. Making a choice each day to dedicate your relationship to love enhances its presence and keeps you on the right track.

Peace: The way to peace is through surrendering to the presence of love. By joining together you bypass the conflict that occurs when you try to stay separate, and you acknowledge that in truth there is only one being in the relationship.

Trust: To trust is a leap of faith, which requires you to let go of the need to control or manipulate the relationship. The greater the trust the greater the level of safety that is established, allowing for deeper intimacy, honesty and partnership.

Abundance: Developing an abundance mentality allows you to grow and relax at the same time. True abundance is enjoyed by appreciating and valuing what you share and by letting go of thoughts of lack or scarcity.

Synergy: True partnership comes about as a result of creative co-operation and focusing on win/win thinking. This enables the relationship to move forward as a powerful unit, contributing good to the world.

Complimentary medicine!

How often do we take the time to give our partners a genuine compliment? When we get caught up in the busyness of life we can forget to tell them how much we appreciate them, care about them, value them and love them. The three most powerful words in the English language are 'I love you'. We might say them a lot in the early period of a relationship, but once that wears off we have a tendency to save them up for special occasions. I have even known people express the fear that if they tell their partner how much they love them regularly then the words will lose their meaning. This erroneous belief is the ego's attempt to prevent us from enjoying the benefits of true love. The giving of compliments is a loving act. Our deepest human need is to feel valued and appreciated so to give sincere compliments is a way to feed and nourish the relationship.

Complimentary medicine can take several forms. There is the verbal option of telling your partner what you appreciate in them, from their culinary skills through to their love for you. A loving exercise is to sit opposite each other and use the words, 'Something I appreciate about you is . . .', going back and forth. This is particularly useful if you have been experiencing difficulty in your relationship, as it connects you to the presence of love. An enjoyable way to express your appreciation is to give your partner surprise treats. Buying them small presents, taking them breakfast in bed or planning a day out are all ideas that contribute to the growth of the relationship.

Having fun

Are you having fun yet? It is easy to become too serious with the dominance of the work ethic in our culture. In our efforts to have a good relationship we may work very hard at it while forgetting to enjoy the process. Through committing to fun you open yourself to being spontaneous, carefree, joyful and playful. These might not seem particularly grown-up qualities, but this is even more reason to employ them wholeheartedly!

We all have a playful side to our character. Letting it out in a relationship brings us closer together. As the comedian Victor Borge said, 'Laughter is the shortest distance between two people.' If you experience resistance to having fun, talking about it together helps you to become clear about your past conditioning. Did your parents have fun in their relationship, or is your memory dominated by thoughts of conflict, struggle and disagreement? Often people feel that they need to give themselves permission to start having fun again.

One of the ways that Veronica and I have fun is to go camping. We gain a wonderful sense of freedom from throwing all our gear in the back of the car and heading off on an adventure. Once in New Zealand we had borrowed an ancient tent from a friend and all we had was an army knife and one small pot to do our cooking. I still laugh as I remember trying to cook dinner while surrounded by people with sophisticated barbecues and luxurious camper homes! Still, it's the fun that counts. Take up rollerblading, rent bicycles for a day, have a stock of games, go to comedy clubs, tell each other jokes. Make a list of all the things that would encourage you to have fun together and schedule them into your calendar.

Focusing on friendship

The greatest gift in my relationship with Veronica is that she's my closest friend. We are always happiest when we are relating to each other as friends. Making your friendship a priority is an essential ingredient in a loving relationship. One way to develop this is to be celibate for a period of time. Some close friends of mine, Kim and Didier, decided to be celibate for the first three months of their relationship. This gave them the space to get to know each other without the increased intensity of sexual intimacy. The ninety-day period seemed to help clear out the effects of their past relationships so that they could be really present together; several years on they enjoy one of the happiest relationships I know.

Becoming sexually involved accelerates the intensity of a relationship as it stimulates a greater level of intimacy. Intimacy can be read as 'in-to-me-see', meaning that someone sees into the core of your being. This can activate the fear of being vulnerable and cause you to shut off. Taking the opportunity to develop a friendship first creates a greater sense of safety for handling increased intimacy. If you have been in a relationship for a period of time, then choosing to be celibate can help reconnect and deepen the friendship.

It is very helpful to make friendship a priority when you are experiencing difficulties in a relationship. At these times you can set your partner up as your enemy. Certainly the last thing they feel like is a friend; they appear to be out to cause you misery and distress. You forget why you got together in the first place and you entertain thoughts of separation. By making friendship a priority you put the wellbeing of each other first and you stop attacking one another. As a friend you want the other person to be happy, which might even mean that you let go of the relationship. Having the courage to embrace this possibility, coming from a place of true friendship, returns the relationship to love.

Setting your partner free

This idea can be a challenge to apply but I believe helps a relationship to stay fresh and vibrant. I have observed many relationships damaged by the level of possessiveness, jealousy and control that can govern the partnership. It takes courage and trust to set your partner free. The key is to develop clear communication and to make each other's happiness more important than the outcome of the relationship.

There are two primary states that inhibit the development of freedom. The first state is that of dependency. Symptoms of dependency include having a sense of neediness and reliance on your partner for your identity and confidence; feeling as if you are unable to make decisions without your partner; feeling possessive within the relationship if your partner asserts their individuality, and feeling guilty if you assert yours.

The second state is the flip side of dependency, which is the state of independence. The primary characteristic of independence is the need to be in control. If you are an independent person you will find it difficult to let in love and support because it is perceived as a threat. You keep up a barrier between yourself and your partner which controls the level of intimacy you experience. In our culture achieving independence has been believed to be the major goal of a relationship, but in fact it is based on a fear of surrendering to true partnership.

Moving through dependence and independence allows you to reach a state of interdependence. This is when you experience freedom in a relationship because it is based on mutual respect, trust and internal security. Having interdependence creates a synergistic relationship. Synergy means that the whole is greater than the sum of its parts. To have synergy is to experience that, as a relationship, you are greater together than as two separate individuals. In order for synergy to occur you need to be willing to have creative co-operation. This takes you away from your comfort zones and gives the relationship a spirit of adventure as you blaze your own trail into the unknown.

Letting go of the future

How many times have you sabotaged a relationship by projecting into the future and making a decision based on the resulting fear? As soon as you worry about the future you are out of present time. By letting go of the future you can experience the truth about a relationship, for fear will cloud your perception. I have to smile as I look back over the number of relationships I rejected as a result of fearing the future: I would go out on a date and within an hour I was trying to work out the future: what was going to happen, what were the implications, was it going to lead to marriage and kids or just an enjoyable evening?

Take a moment to look at your relationship fears about the future. They might include the fear of rejection, a loss of freedom, feeling trapped or controlled, financial difficulties, expectations, roles and responsibilities. At some stage you have to make the leap of faith, otherwise you continue to let fear rule, which stops you following your heart. As you begin to trust the future you relax and become peaceful. You see things as they really are. Since the future is a projection of your own mind, by changing your mind about it you create a new world for yourself.

Going beyond your limits

We all have fears, doubts and insecurities but do not need to limit ourselves by letting these feelings dominate our relationships. Being willing to go beyond your past limits allows you discover the full potential of your relationship – you might be in for a wonderful surprise!

I have seen many people talk themselves out of a relationship before they have even entered one. Hannah came to me desperately searching for a relationship. In her early thirties, she had been single for seven years, as the result of a difficult past relationship and through putting her energies into her career. She confided that what she wanted more than anything else in life was to have a loving relationship and children. It was such a major step for her just to reveal this that she cried with relief. She had felt so ashamed to want this; she saw it as a weakness and felt that she should be OK on her own, that she shouldn't need anyone. She had built up an independent lifestyle that was now proving a factor limiting her happiness. When I reassured her that it was natural to want a relationship and family, and that it was not necessarily a sign of being dependent on another, she cheered up considerably.

The first step for Hannah was to go out and meet people. Having absorbed herself in her work she had avoided socialising. Gradually she started to accept people's invitations instead of making excuses. Each time she went out she felt as if she was breaking through an old fear or doubt and it became easier to meet men. To continue her progress she needed to become more honest about what she wanted in relationships. By stating that you are ready and available for a relationship you set a clear intention. By avoiding your real feelings you will continue to repeat past patterns. When men approached her Hannah told them she wanted a relationship. Men who found this threatening hastily retreated and she could get to know those who were really interested. By being clear, you avoid the game-playing that can limit a relationship. Finally Hannah did meet a man who was ready and available. She continued to transcend her limits by starting the relationship slowly, building a friendship and letting go of her fears of the future.

If you are already in a relationship you can rejuvenate it by discovering the limits that you have imposed on it. If you have certain roles or habitual responses, experiment by making changes. Do you always sleep on the same side of the bed? If so, try exchanging sides and notice how it feels. Are you the financial planner and organiser? Swap these roles and discover that you are both capable of handling the finances. Do you do all the cooking, shopping and household chores? If so, share these roles or bring in some extra help. Going beyond your limits keeps you learning and actively engaged in life.

Having faith!

Picture a doctor's waiting room. This doctor is no ordinary doctor: he specialises in healing relationship conditions. In the waiting room there are a number of people suffering from a variety of ailments. One person is grieving the loss of a relationship, another is searching for a relationship, another is struggling in a relationship and yet another is caught in the middle of two relationships. As their number is called they go and see the doctor. To each one the doctor gives different advice, but the final prescription he gives them is the same. Written in big bold letters are the words 'HAVE FAITH'.

It takes great courage and personal strength to have faith in relationships. The bottom line is that no matter how enlightened you are, 'sh!t happens!' You are going to be hit by challenges and obstacles along the way, and it will be your level of faith that determines whether you rise to these challenges or give up. After my first major relationship ended, I was devastated for nearly a year. I was tempted to quit relationships, as they appeared only to lead to trouble and strife. As I look back now I feel truly thankful for that experience and for all my relationships, since each one has contributed to the rich variety of my life. Every relationship has the potential for love and healing, which rests only upon your commitment to letting go of fear and trusting in the intrinsic value of each encounter.

4

Work in Joy!

Often people try to live their lives backwards: they try to have
more things, or more money, in order to do more of what they
want so that they will be happier. The way it actually works is
the reverse. You must first be who you really are, then do what
you really need to do, in order to have what you want.

Margaret Young

I received a phone call one day from Gary enquiring about
booking some coaching sessions. He was calling on his
mobile phone while on holiday in a French valley, and asked
if I would be able to see him upon his return. He arrived for his
first session late, rushed and out of breath. He launched into a
success story about his busy executive working life. Gary worked
for a large company, travelled the world and earned a good
salary. I was beginning to wonder why he had come to see me! He
then went on to reveal that despite all this apparent success, there
was something missing. Although his work was very stimulating
he had no sense of real enjoyment, true meaning or inspiration.
He claimed that often he just went through the motions at work
and that he kept doing it to pay the bills and keep the security of
his corporate ID. He claimed that one day he would quit and
follow his dream of writing a novel and enjoying a peaceful,
relaxing lifestyle. In the meantime he believed that he had to keep
his head down and keep advancing until he had accumulated
enough resources to take an early retirement.

Gary's story is not unique. For many of us, our experience of
work is defined by the amount of effort and struggle we put in
each day. We work long hours in soulless environments to prove
our worth in a competitive and tough world. The idea of work

being fun, enjoyable and profitable, both financially and spiritually, seems a remote fantasy. If you relate to this picture then it's time to ring the changes. This doesn't mean you should hand in your resignation first thing tomorrow morning. What I extend to you is the invitation to change your beliefs and attitude in order to transform your experience of work. In particular, reflect on the meaning and purpose you have given your work so that you can create true success in your working life.

HUMAN BEING OR HUMAN DOING?

When I ask audiences for the first thought they have upon awakening each day, the most common answer is, 'What have I got to do today?' The 'to do' list has become a modern bible, which people use to measure their lives. Often, we convince ourselves that our obsession with our 'to do' list is temporary – that once we have completed the list we will enjoy our lives. The trouble is that the way we tend to reward ourselves for getting through the list is to make another one! Obviously there is great value in doing things and having clear objectives. The point I am stressing is that by making 'doing' a greater priority than 'being' we face the danger of letting our lives get out of balance. (Even when we die, our 'to do' list will not have been completed!)

Ten key principles provide the context in which to make the shift to putting 'being' before 'doing'. By aligning yourself with these timeless principles for true success, you ensure that your actions and communications are balanced and effective. We will now take a look at each principle in turn and explore how we can apply it in our working lives.

Love

> Work is love made visible. *Kahlil Gibran*

We aspire to do the work we love and love the work we do. Those who are fortunate enough to be in that position regard work as a blessing, a gift and an opportunity to enhance and contribute to the lives of others. When work is an expression of love, it embodies our deepest values and hopes. Work is no longer an activity that removes us from our lives, but a daily reminder to come back to our hearts. True motivation comes from this ocean of love that is constantly full and flowing.

Unfortunately we tend not to associate the word 'love' with work. In fact it's probably one of the last words to be used in the workplace. Somewhere in our evolution we have split love and work, putting them in different compartments of our lives. We mistakenly believe that when we discover what we love to do, we can then unite love and work in our lives. This is backward thinking. It is when we decide to bring love into our work, whatever type of work we do, that we experience the joy of love and work combined.

When we do have the courage to bring love into the workplace it makes work a deeply rewarding experience. When love is absent, time drags, struggle prevails and drudgery is the name of the game. See if you can remember a time when you experienced love at work. Maybe it came in the form of support received from a colleague, a heartfelt thank-you from a customer or an opportunity to contribute to someone's life. There is no greater gift than that of love. Every day, in every way we can give that gift by opening our hearts, focusing on how we can help and extending beyond our limited perceptions of ourselves. As Joseph Campbell movingly put it, 'When we quit thinking primarily about ourselves and our own self-preservation, we undergo a truly heroic transformation of consciousness'.

Exercise: Think about how you can bring love into your work each day.

Integrity

It is not who is right, but what is right, that is of importance. *Thomas Huxley*

The *Oxford English Dictionary* defines integrity as wholeness, soundness, uprightness and honesty. Imagine how it would be to hold yourself to those attributes in your work. So often we are tempted to tell a white lie or paint a pretty picture in order to make a quick sale, fix a problem or get out of a tricky situation. As long as we behave in this fashion, we will not experience the deep sense of joy and fulfilment that derives from having integrity in our work. In the long term it damages our business relationships, as trust and co-operation break down. To have integrity means having the courage to follow your conscience, stand by your word and have consistency in your actions.

I witnessed the effects of allowing integrity to fall by the wayside, in a training programme I ran for a sales team. Productivity was down and a rift was growing between the team and the manager. The team said that they had reached a stage where they feared the manager, whose frequent outbursts of anger and apparent lack of understanding were detrimental to the team's effectiveness. From the manager I heard the other side of the story. He was feeling highly stressed through being accountable for a large amount of profit for the company. His seniors were breathing down his neck and as a result he feared for the team's position. When I asked him what he valued, he replied that integrity was the principle he strove for. He felt that it had slipped due to the increased pressure. He realised that he needed to recommit to his integrity, which meant to re-establish communication with the team and to focus his attention on meeting their needs. He knew that if they felt supported then they would perform well, which would increase productivity.

> **Exercise:** If you worked with absolute integrity, how would you work differently?

Authenticity

> Maybe being oneself is always an acquired taste. *Patricia Hampl*

How often do you experience your true, genuine self in the workplace? To be able to answer this question presupposes that you already know who your authentic self is. A barometer by which to measure this is the amount of peace you experience. If you feel peaceful on a regular basis then you are being authentic. If you often feel stressed, fearful or oppressed at work then you are hiding your true self by acting a role without putting your heart and soul into it.

You might be playing the role of a good employee, boss or partner but without your heart and soul it is a meaningless task. Letting go of acting a role is a choice to go beyond your fears and risk letting others experience the real you. People often disclose the fear that they will be perceived as a rebel if they choose to be authentic. Being a rebel though is just another role and certainly doesn't bring you peace. I had a client who worked for a company which insisted that all male employees wear suits. He resented this policy because since he worked for an internal department and didn't meet customers or suppliers, he felt that it would be fair to have a relaxed dress code. One day a month they had a dress-down day, when if people chose, they could make a donation to charity and dress casually. He said that he would happily make a donation every day to be able to wear what he wanted so that he could be himself. I pointed out that the challenge to be authentic didn't lie in what clothes he wore, but in his intention to let his real self shine through, whatever clothing or environment he was in.

> **Exercise:** See if you can remember a time when you were your authentic self at work. How was it and what happened? Commit to being your authentic self.

Compassion

> Our lives will always be full if our hearts are always giving.
> *Anonymous*

There is an inspiring story recounted in *Chicken Soup for the Soul at Work*, of a man who had always wanted to be a cartoonist but never knew how to go about it. One day he wrote to the host of a television show about cartoons asking for guidance. A few weeks later he received a helpful letter from the host pointing him in the right direction. He followed this advice but soon gave up after being rejected by a variety of different publications. Over a year later he received a further letter from the host saying that he hoped things were going well and wishing him lots of luck. This act of compassion encouraged the cartoonist to make another attempt to sell his sketches. These ideas went on to become 'Dilbert', the famous cartoon character of Scott Adams.

When we bring compassion into our work, not only does it transform our own working experience it also touches the lives of others around us. Compassion creates a ripple effect with no logical end. Compassion arises from the understanding that as human beings we all have similar experiences – we all have our ups and downs, hopes and fears, pains and joy, loneliness and friendship. Compassion is the choice to be led by our hearts rather than by judgement. It is the ultimate act of choosing love over fear.

The voice of fear tells us that to be compassionate in the workplace is a sign of weakness: if we are compassionate we will be walked over, taken advantage of, made the scapegoat and will fail in our aspirations. In fact these symptoms are the effects of low self-esteem, and extending compassion to yourself and others reclaims your lost self-worth and belief. I have experienced this in relation to having to handle several outstanding payments from clients. Whenever I have tried to resolve the dilemma by taking a hard approach motivated by fear, I have been met with hostility and resentment. When I have extended compassion by seeking to understand the client's financial difficulty and offered to help in advising on how to overcome it, I have experienced a tremendous shift in their willingness to pay and received their appreciation for being caring.

To be compassionate is to experience our essential nature as human beings. It is a sure sign that someone has lost their way when they are behaving without compassion. If you are working for or with someone who behaves in this way, put yourself in their shoes. You begin to understand their fear and pain, which inhibit the natural expression of their love. When your compassion is feeling blocked ask yourself, 'What is the fear that is preventing me from opening my heart?' By committing yourself to love, you will find the joy of compassion returning to your work.

Creativity

> Great improvisers are like priests. They are thinking only
> of their God. *Stéphane Grappelli*, jazz violinist

I spent my life between the ages of five and eighteen studiously learning the violin. I took a year out before attending music college and went to live on a kibbutz in Israel. There was a jazz band on the kibbutz and for the first time in my life I played without sheet music and had to improvise as I went along. It came as a great shock to find that I could hardly play once the music had been taken away! I realised that through the process of receiving a high level of training, a certain element of creativity had been knocked out of me. I witnessed other musicians with less formal training than myself able to be creative and spontaneous in their playing.

In today's climate companies have to rely on employees to be innovative and creative to respond to the high level of change in the workplace. Yet these very same workers have often been so highly trained that the creative spark has been extinguished. Often they have to unlearn their previous training for their creative skills to thrive.

The Latin root of the word create is *creare*, meaning 'to bring into being'. It is in our nature to imagine, dream, invent and shape our world. We are all creative beings who need to give ourselves permission to unleash the creativity within. As we focus on our creativity and remove our past conditioning, we will discover creative ideas and energy, and the means to bring these ideas into physical reality. When our work is infused with creativity there is a sense of being in the flow of life. Coincidence and synchronicity become daily occurrences: you find yourself thinking of someone and they call; you are in need of a contact and by a fortuitous route it appears; somebody presents you with the information that moves you forward with a project. This natural flow is always available. When you open yourself to your creativity, you open yourself to this current that is within you and your life.

> **Exercise:** If you were to put creativity and your creative ideas at the centre stage of your working life, how would your work be different?

Abundance

> Do what you love and the money will follow. *Marsha Sinetar* (author of the book of the same title)

Abundance is not about having an accumulation of financial wealth – true abundance is a state of mind. It is an attitude that acknowledges the fact that there is plenty of work, money, love and opportunity to support everyone. To be abundant is to give and receive freely. Abundance flows out of a deep inner sense of personal worth and security. It enables you to follow your heart and share your success with others. The most abundant people I know are the most generous people I know. To be generous is not just to give money; it encompasses the sharing of time, information, resources and love.

An inspiring example can be seen in a client of mine called Sylvia. Whenever the financial side of her business slips, she calls me up for a 'prosperity dinner' and we go out to celebrate her abundance. By focusing on what she already has, she breaks through any thoughts of lack and scarcity which feed feelings of fear and insecurity.

Most people are conditioned to believe that there is not enough to go around: that you have to hold on to what you've got. These beliefs create a mentality of scarcity, which causes us to compete with each other, withhold information and resources and celebrate the failure of others. We mistakenly believe that the failure of others contributes to our own success. Some people even put more energy into bringing others down than into building their own lives. Ultimately, living with a belief in lack either causes us to end up with nothing, or to be terrified of losing what we have.

Being abundant in our work is a commitment to stretch ourselves beyond thoughts of lack and scarcity. Start to celebrate the successes of others by learning from their accomplishments and creations. Using them as inspiration supports our own success by showing us what is possible.

> **Exercise:** My blocks to being abundant are . . . Write down your responses and commit to clearing these limiting beliefs.

Service

> I don't know what your destiny will be, but one thing I know: the only ones of you who will be truly happy will be those of you have sought and found how to serve. *Albert Schweitzer*, philanthropist

To whom would you give a larger tip: the waiter who served you with warmth, respect, care and consideration or the waiter who served you with lack of interest and a brusque manner? Eating in a restaurant is a direct way of experiencing the effects of service. It always bemuses me when I am served with a casual attitude when there is such a direct correlation between the quality of service and the reward received. If you are in a salaried position then the quality of your service doesn't appear to have such a direct impact on your return, although the true nature of service goes far beyond measurement by money.

A sense of service stems from the desire to help others coupled with the understanding that by helping others you are helping yourself. There are several myths about service that prevent us from giving fully. The main one is that service involves some form of sacrifice, whether it is of time, money, effort or expertise. There is a world of difference between service and sacrifice. Service is based on a genuine calling to contribute and make a difference to the lives of others. Sacrifice stems from the mis-understanding that in order to 'do good' you must deprive yourself of something of value. You can tell the difference by noticing the outcomes of your actions. If you truly serve then you give of the best of yourself and feel joyous and fulfilled. When you give out of sacrifice you feel depleted, drained and unfulfilled. To truly serve requires you to look after your own needs as well as the needs of others. I know that I cannot be so effective in my work if I have sacrificed my own needs to help another; the greatest way I can be of service is to retreat into my own world and take care of my own self before recommitting to being of service in the world.

Another false notion is that you must leave the commercial world if you are to serve. This is formed on the belief that service and money do not go together and that service is limited to the voluntary/charity sector. Thankfully we are waking up to the realisation that in the commercial sector it is essential to serve with a heart.

By making our work a form of service we give ourselves the gift of fulfilment through commitment to supporting others. We will come to know the truth in the words of the Indian poet Rabindranath Tagore, 'I slept and dreamt that life was joy, I awoke and saw that life was service, I acted and behold, service was joy' (from *I Won't Let You Go: Selected Poems*).

> **Exercise:** If you saw your work as service, what would you be doing differently, how would it feel? What contribution would you be making?

Vision

> You are what your deep driving desire is. As your desire is, so is your will. As your will is, so is your deed. As your deed is, so is your destiny. *Brihadaranyaka Upanishad*, IV.4.5

Would you describe yourself as having been a daydreamer as a child? Did you enjoy creating futuristic pictures in your mind about how your life was going to map out? Unfortunately this ability tends to get inhibited as we are taught to grow up, be realistic and responsible. We put our dreams on hold and get on with the serious business of working for a living. If this has been the case for you, then it is time to give yourself permission to start dreaming again and to recover a sense of possibility. Unless you live in a state of vision, you are letting your past run your future. You have to be willing to see the future as different from the past in order to welcome a state of vision. Just because something happened yesterday does not mean that it's going to happen today. As you start to let go of your past conditioning you open yourself to the possibilities that exist in the here and now.

All vision starts with the seed of an idea planted in the back of the mind. As we nurture the idea by imagining it coming into fruition, we lay the foundations for the actualisation of the idea. One of the major blocks to allowing ourselves to live in a state of vision is the question, 'How am going to achieve it?' In my workshops I encourage people to put their doubting mind on hold so that they can first look at the question of vision. By separating the vision from the how of creating it, people can open the door again to their imagination.

Another block is caused by feelings of guilt and unworthiness. This is a form of self-sabotage, which is common for people who feel that they do not deserve to live their vision. They associate vision with being selfish, arrogant and self-centred so they give up on their dreams before they have even had a chance to picture them.

One of my dreams was to write a book. I had never been a grade A English student at school so I looked at other people's books with envy and caution. I didn't believe that I had the capability to realise this idea. However, encouraged by the fact that many of my friends are authors, I began to study the formula for writing a book. First of all it requires you to have an idea of what you are going to write about; then you work on creating the proposal to show the publishers. I put a synopsis of a book together with chapter outlines, marketing plans and my profile. I had the support of Louise Manson, a journalist and friend, and together we submitted the proposal. It was an extraordinary feeling when I was offered a contract. I then had to face the task of writing the book – alone! The book that you have in your hands is living proof that it *is* possible to realise a vision.

I had the opportunity while growing up at the Yehudi Menuhin School to witness Lord Menuhin's visionary gifts. The school developed out of his dream to provide a nurturing environment for musical children. He also founded a charity, Live Music Now! which provides the opportunity for young musicians to take music into community settings such as hospitals, schools, prisons and homes for the elderly. The following words, drawn from his writings, captures the spirit of his vision:

> As a small child, playing the violin, my naïve dream was to be able thereby to heal the suffering heart . . . Ever since I can remember I have tried to relate the beauty of great music to the harmony of life . . . I even imagined that if I could play the Chaconne of Bach inspiringly enough in the Sistine Chapel under the eyes of Michelangelo, all that is ignoble and vile would miraculously disappear from our world!

Who are the people in your life who have followed their dreams and realised their vision? There is a passage in the Bible that says: "Where there is no vision, the people perish.' It is essential for your wellbeing and happiness to live with vision. There will be obstacles along the way, but by focusing on your vision you will ride the challenges to reach greater and greater heights.

Exercise: If you had no fear or guilt, what would your vision for your work be?

Purpose

> Once you learn what your life is about there is no way to erase the knowledge. No matter how afraid you become you have no choice. If you try to do something different

with your life, you will always sense there is something missing. *James Redfield*, author of *The Celestine Prophecy*.

What is the purpose of your work? Is it to gain the approval of others, to earn enough money to pay the bills, to prove that you are good enough? Or is it to have fun, to serve with a sense of love and compassion, to live your vision? The purpose of your work is something that you can choose. This replaces the idea many people have that there is some divine purpose waiting to be revealed to them. Ultimately the meaning that your work has will be the meaning you give to it. If you want your work to be an opportunity to express your true self and to be a platform for the expression of your talents while contributing to the lives of others, then it will be. If you want your work just to give you the means by which you survive from Monday to Friday, it will do that too. The choice lies in your hands.

To make the right choice for yourself you need to follow your inner knowing and wisdom: the gut feeling that you have about what is true for you. This requires you to peel away the layers of conditioning you have received about work. What lies behind why you do what you do? If your work is motivated by fear, guilt, competition and sacrifice, it is a clear sign that you are not following your purpose. If you leave your work feeling drained, disheartened, frustrated and blocked then you are not 'on purpose'. If, on the other hand, love, authenticity, a desire to give and serve inspire your motivation for work then you are on purpose. If you feel energised, rewarded, fulfilled and at peace within your work, then you are following your purpose.

It is a joy and an inspiration to observe people who are on purpose in their working lives. They exude an enthusiasm and strength that only comes when you do what you love and love what you do. When I was a musician I received lessons from an extraordinary man called Hans Keller. A survivor of the Holocaust, Hans was a chain-smoker who suffered from a degenerative disease of the spine. He could hardly sit upright in his chair, but when music was played he came to life. His greatest teaching was the inspiration he spread from his love of music. Many musicians continue to play long into their old age since the expression of music is the purpose of their life. Lord Menuhin's diary was still full of engagements to conduct and teach at the moment of his untimely death. Who do you know who inspires you with their commitment to follow their purpose?

There is a Sanskrit word *dharma*, one of the meanings of which is 'purpose in life'. Dharma means that we have unique talents and unique ways of expressing those talents. When we combine our unique gifts with a spirit of service then we will be on purpose in our lives. To discover your purpose, simply ask yourself the following questions: what would you like the purpose of your work to be? How are you best suited to serve humanity? What are your unique talents that you love to express? Listen carefully to the answers. Notice the temptation to edit the ideas you get, especially if they appear far-fetched or unrealistic. Write your responses down and commit to the possibility of letting your work be an expression of your purpose.

Appreciation

> The deepest principle in human nature is the craving to be appreciated. *William James*, philospher and psychologist

At The Happiness Project one of the fundamental ideas that we teach about the working environment is, 'A happy workforce is a productive workforce'. The key to creating and maintaining a happy workforce is to value and appreciate people. We have become experts at giving constructive criticism and feedback, but how often do we prioritise the giving of genuine appreciation and thanks?

Second only to money, the desire to be recognised and valued is the major reason why people turn up to work. Without appreciation, work is an incomplete loop: it feels as if we are left hanging in mid-air. Resentment creeps in, trust breaks down and communication suffers if there is not a complete cycle of acknowledgement. We are human beings, not machines; we are fed by the appreciation we receive from others, and in return we perform well. Our conditioning has led us to look for the mistakes in ourselves and others, rather than to focus on what we and others are doing right. We are often quicker to blame than to praise, under the mistaken assumption that by making someone feel bad about themselves, we will get them to deliver what we want. I don't know about you, but I respond far more effectively when I am encouraged and praised rather than blamed and criticised.

In many work environments the belief seems to be that the need for appreciation is a sign of weakness and insecurity; that we shouldn't need to rely on others for positive feedback, as if doing the work itself is enough of a reason to perform well. Imagine being in an intimate relationship in which your partner never gave you any direct appreciation. Would you want to be the very best that you could be if you weren't appreciated? There is a misguided fear in the workplace that if we start appreciating people the need for appreciation will be a bottomless pit. The irony is that in fact our appreciation quota does not take long to be filled. The way to break the pattern is to be the one to start to give appreciation: a spoken thank-you, a note of gratitude, an e-mail of encouragement, a small gift of recognition. Never miss an opportunity to spread sincere appreciation. As Meister Eckhart, the Dominican theologian, declared: 'If the only prayer you say in your whole life is "thank you," that would suffice.'

When I work with a team on building its team spirit, the turning point often comes when people are invited to give appreciation to each other. I have witnessed teams in which communication had broken down, and mistrust ruled, transformed by the power of appreciation. Tom Peters, the management guru, captures the essence of this in his statement, 'Celebrate what you want to see more of.' The challenge lies in implementing this strategy at times of difficulty. It's obviously easier to celebrate when things are going well, but pointing out what is working in stressful situations lifts people's morale and increases their motivation to turn things around.

Applying these principles in your working life helps you to make the leap from human doing to human being. This opens the door for your work to be an expression of love rather than an act of labour. As well as these principles the following ideas are integral components of expressing joy at work.

Clearing Your Conditioning

Your conditioning is the sum total of the beliefs, attitudes and opinions that you have absorbed throughout your life. The conditioning you have received about work colours your outlook and may contain elements that are not useful or true for you. If so, then raising your awareness allows you to make new choices which liberate you from limiting factors and enhance your personal effectiveness.

I have observed five primary unhelpful beliefs that dominate people's views of work. As we consider them, see which ones you resonate with, and give yourself the opportunity to make new choices.

The source of happiness in work lies outside myself

As someone who is self-employed, I am very aware that if I am unhappy in my work, I am fully responsible for figuring out why and deciding what I can do about it. For those who are employed and unhappy in their work, there may be a tendency to place the responsibility on their boss, team or company and blame them for their unhappiness. A habit that is shared by both the self-employed and the employed is that if they are unhappy in their work, they start looking elsewhere, believing that the grass is greener in other pastures. The truth is that the source of happiness in work lies within yourself and it is your responsibility to make the changes necessary to create enjoyable and fulfilling work.

I am aware that this can be a challenging idea for those people who experience genuinely difficult relationships and situations in the workplace. However, as long as you place the source of your happiness outside yourself, you play a victim role which prevents you from moving forward. The key to your freedom and happiness in work lies in your willingness to take full responsibility.

The greatest obstacle to this is the fear of change. The irony is that although we fear change, the one certainty in life is that change is inevitable. Understanding the nature of change enables us to feel more confident about responding to it. Since we now live in a work culture where the capacity to manage change successfully is top of the agenda, our ability to respond to it in creative and resourceful ways is crucial if we are to thrive and prosper.

In all the cases I have seen, once someone has moved through their fear of change, they have enjoyed greater happiness. If you are unhappy in your work, the first step is to recognise that the decision to be happy is one that only you can make. I counselled a lady who claimed that she was unhappy working as a personal assistant for the director of a music company. She said that she had an inspiring and fair boss, who liked to work hard and play hard. She discussed how her role was constantly evolving and growing within the company and said that she enjoyed working with the other staff and interacting with the musicians. I was perplexed about where the source of her unhappiness lay, until she admitted that saying she was unhappy was a habit she had acquired since so many of her friends complained about their work. In fact she was afraid of admitting how much she enjoyed her work because of how her friends might respond. The major encouragement she needed was to give herself permission to be happy.

If you work in a culture where complaining abounds, it is an act of courage to declare your happiness. Making a list of what you currently enjoy provides a helpful reminder if you are tempted to revert to the 'Irritable Howl Syndrome', i.e. the chronic desire to moan and complain! Focusing on what you enjoy develops an outlook of valuing and appreciating what you already have in your working life.

In my workshops one of the exercises I use is to discuss who is the happiest person you know, and why. One participant gave the telling example of the caretaker in the locker room at his golf club. He is surrounded by wealthy businessmen who appear to have it all, yet he is the one who radiates happiness and joy. His job is to clean shoes and yet his manner is always open, friendly and optimistic. This demonstrates that happiness lies in your attitude and approach rather than in the type of work you do.

If you are taking responsibility for your happiness and are still genuinely distressed, then be willing to ask for help. Find others who are doing what you would like to do and ask them for guidance. Your willingness to discover what is right and true for you will open doors in a way that you might not have believed possible. This may require you to go out on a limb – but that is where the fruit lies.

Work has to be hard, stressful, a struggle, even a sacrifice

This belief has been heavily influenced by the puritanical work ethic according to which it is only through hard work, and lots of it, that you will be redeemed. You are led to believe that the harder you work, the more stress you experience and the more you sacrifice your personal happiness, then the higher the rewards in the workplace. I was talking to a friend, who is a trader in commercial banking, about the psychological conditioning that dominates his working environment. He disclosed that in his work a job description is not worth the paper it's written on because if you were to follow it you would be out of the job immediately. The unwritten rule is that you have to work long and hard hours and sacrifice your personal life for the company, and if you can't handle the accompanying stress, then tough! He said that there is a high level of cynicism about the idea of working with integrity and authenticity because someone will always come in behind your back to undermine you.

It is not only in the financial world that you encounter this pattern. In my work with doctors, nurses, GPs and healthcare professionals I came across high doses of stress, sacrifice and long hours. Tragically, GPs have one of the highest rates of suicide due to the interminable pressure they experience. The question, 'Who cares for the carer?' arises when the work ethic dominates the caring profession. Musicians and artists too who are influenced by this conditioning. A sense of disillusionment and despondency can result if they have to take on work that goes against their creative flair.

We now work longer hours in Britain than in any other

country in Europe. The trouble is that more doesn't equal better. 'Workaholism' is as big a social problem as alcoholism and needs to be addressed as such. We are waking up to this fact, which was highlighted by one manager I spoke with recently. He declared: 'If I am going to spend more time with this team than with my own wife and kids, then I am going to make sure that the quality of relationships and the work experience is as enjoyable as possible.'

According to the work ethic, enjoyable, creative and inspiring work is not defined as real work. If you do catch yourself enjoying your work then the onslaught of guilt usually knocks you back to the familiar pattern of struggle. The work ethic is driven by the belief that anything worthwhile requires large amounts of effort and strain; it invalidates work that comes easily. The greatest difference between work governed by the work ethic and work governed by your true purpose is the measure of enjoyment you experience. There are still challenges and demands when you are working on purpose, but being clear about your purpose pulls you through all difficulties and causes you to learn and grow from the experiences.

Exercise: To evaluate how much you are influenced by the work ethic reflect on the following statements:

I prefer Monday morning to Friday evening
True/False

My lifestyle can be summed up in three easily defined ways: work, more work and even more work.
True/False

I put work before my relationships, health and leisure.
True/False

I regard high anxiety and feeling stressed out as normal states at work.
True/False

If I wake early, I use the time to work rather than relax.
True/False

I work over 48 hours a week.
True/False

I regard people who leave work on time as part-timers.
True/False

I would compromise my integrity in order to 'get ahead' in work.
True/False

I like others to know how hard I work.
True/False

I think a little less of God for taking a day of rest!
True/False

If you gave more *true* than *false* answers, you need to make some new choices for yourself with regard to your current attitude about work. Below are a list of life-enhancing beliefs to undo the conditioning that work has to be hard, stressful, a struggle and a sacrifice. Pick any that seem helpful, and create some of your own to increase your personal effectiveness.

◆ Work is a source of creativity and inspiration.
◆ Work can serve me.
◆ Work nourishes and supports me.
◆ I can excel and enjoy my work.
◆ I can be relaxed and a high achiever.
◆ Being on purpose in my work supports everyone.
◆ I deserve to enjoy my work.
◆ Work affirms my true self.
◆ Work can help me grow spiritually and emotionally.
◆ I discover inspiration and joy in my work.

Your work defines who you are

Picture this: arriving at a party you meet a variety of people. Invariably the opening line is 'Hello, and what do you do?' If you do something that meets the approval of other people you feel important and accepted. If you do something that doesn't meet others' expectations, you feel like a nobody.

Work has come to define who you are: the more successful you are in your work, the more importance and value you have in the eyes of the world. As long as your identity is linked to your work, your sense of self-worth is open to being tossed around like a ship without sails on the high seas.

Unfortunately in our education system it is rare to find teachers who encourage young people to discover their unique gifts and talents. It is far more common to find students forced to fit into a regime that suits the minority who are skilled at exams. Parents are caught in the fear of their children not succeeding and therefore push their offspring to conform. This is an understandable scenario but it fails to leave room for young people to grasp who they really are.

Being driven by this belief means that you are constantly trying to prove yourself in the world by what you do. As long as your motivation for work is to prove something, you will rely on other people's opinion of what you do more than you value your own experience of who you are in your work. Your self-esteem and self-confidence will feel threatened because you are placing the source of your worth outside of yourself. The truth is that you have nothing to prove and you are OK exactly as you are. By integrating this way of thinking into your working life you start relying on your own inner strength rather than looking for the approval of others.

The accumulation of money and financial survival are the major reasons for work

The most successful and wealthy people I have met do not work for the money. Now I know you can say that they probably don't need to work for the money! That is true, but when I ask them what is the real reason they work, they declare that it is for the love, passion and enjoyment of their work – and the money follows as a by-product. One person I spoke with, who is worth an estimated £150 million, could have floated his company and doubled his money but decided against it because he loves his involvement in the work.

When I make the accumulation of money my primary motivation for work I am left feeling empty, as if something is missing – and the fact is that something *is* missing: my heart and soul. Whatever your financial position, the commitment to involving your whole being in your work makes what you do a rewarding experience. The result is that you enjoy what you do, perform a better job and are financially remunerated for your contribution.

It is not wrong to be motivated by money. Far from it: money is a valuable asset, which brings great joy and freedom of choice into your life. It is when you make money the main reason for working that you come off track. David Myers is a social psychologist who has collated much of the recent research on the relationship between material wealth and personal happiness. In his study, *The Pursuit of Happiness*, he concludes:

> Whether we base our conclusions on self-reported happiness, [or] rates of depression . . . our becoming better off over the last 30 years has not been accompanied by one iota of increased happiness and life satisfaction. It is shocking, because it contradicts our society's materialistic assumptions, but how can we ignore the hard truth: once beyond poverty, further economic growth does not appreciably improve human morale. Making more money, the aim of so many graduates and other dreamers of the 1980s, does not breed bliss.

Resolving your relationship to money frees you from either constantly struggling for financial survival or pinning your happiness on accumulating it. Some of the most common unhelpful beliefs about money are:

◆ Money is the root of all evil.

- Money corrupts.
- It's wrong to have a lot of money when there is so much suffering in the world.
- Money is the source of anxiety and unhappiness.
- You cannot do what you love and be well paid for it.

The truth is that money is innocent! Money has never done anything to harm or damage anyone. It is our conditioning about money that has undesirable consequences. When greed, scarcity or the desire for control drives our behaviour, damaging outcomes can emerge. Money is simply currency that we use as a means of exchange.

> **Exercise:** What are the reasons why you work? If you think that money is the major reason take a look to see what money brings you. For example it may bring you peace of mind, security, happiness and choice. By realising that these are the real reasons you go to work, you take the emphasis off money and place it on the values that connect you with your purpose.

Competition and scarcity rule the workplace

The belief that there isn't enough gives rise to more fear and insecurity than any other form of conditioning. It is an erroneous belief: we live in a universe of plenty. In monetary terms alone the estimated financial wealth of the planet is over £10 million billion – enough for everyone to be a millionaire.

People hesitate to make the leap away from scarcity thinking and competitive behaviour to the belief in abundance and co-operation, because they want to see the evidence that it works first. This is backward thinking, because you will not see the evidence until you believe it! You have to trust and take the step forward first.

I have watched this transition take place in the world of personal development. When I started working in the field there were relatively few seminars and practitioners. People were protective of their databases and contacts, as they were afraid other people would take away their business. As the field has grown there are now countless seminars, practitioners, books and products. As a result, rather than business becoming more competitive, there is now greater opportunity and synergy between companies than ever before. It is estimated that over one third of adults in the UK are interested in personal development and have either read a book or visited a practitioner. There are now more registered alternative health practitioners in this country than there are GPs. Through co-operative working, business has increased rather than decreased.

To co-operate is to constantly seek mutual benefit in all interactions. It is to extend yourself beyond any beliefs of limitation and lack. You willingly embrace the idea that there is enough for everyone and that one person's success is not achieved at the expense or exclusion of the success of anyone else. Embodying this belief means that you are genuinely able to celebrate the success of others, which reinforces your own potential for success.

Exercise: How would your work change if you worked with a spirit of co-operation and abundance?

Work takes on a new meaning as we release ourselves from our conditioned beliefs. By developing empowering beliefs about work, we move towards creating true success.

Enjoyment at Work

One of the primary characteristics of people who love the work they do is that they make no major distinction between work and play. You may not yet be in the position of doing the work you love, but your commitment to discovering what is right and true for you opens the door of possibility. When I address the subject of 'Enjoyment in Employment' in workshops there is usually considerable cynicism at the idea of work being an enjoyable activity. In fact the thought of work is literally killing people; this is illustrated by a 1994 report in the *European Heart Journal* which showed that the most common time to suffer a heart attack is 9 a.m. on a Monday morning. If you find yourself dreading Monday mornings, then this is a clear indicator that either you are not doing something you enjoy, or you are of the opinion that you cannot enjoy the work you are doing.

To discover what your current attitude is, write down ten words that you associate with work. For example, work is . . .

- hard
- beneficial
- a necessity
- rewarding
- fun
- social
- exhausting
- challenging
- empowering
- boring

Then write down the statement, 'What work means to me is . . .'

Be honest with yourself as you do this. Since these beliefs create your current reality, outlining them is the first step in letting go of unhelpful conditioning. If you find yourself tempted to judge yourself for what you discover, remember the importance of committing to self-acceptance. Judgement is simply the ego's attempt to sabotage your progress. As Carl Jung, the famous psychologist, said: 'We can't change anything in life unless we accept it' (*Collected Writings of Carl Jung*, ed. Anthony Storr). By accepting any negative past conditioning you make peace with it, which, paradoxically, allows you to change it.

Fran was someone who had built up a negative perception about work. She had always given 110 per cent in her work and yet had never felt fully acknowledged for her level of commitment and expertise. She had been with several different companies over the years and in most cases had left feeling disillusioned and let down. She explained that in interviews they would paint a rosy picture of the company, which matched her expectations of the job content and the culture of the organisation. She was looking for a culture in which people wanted to work together as a team, to have a sense of motivation and encouragement within the team and to be committed to personal development. But when it came to the reality of the work she found that it was the same story of long hours in a competitive atmosphere and if you wanted to do any further training you had to pay for it yourself.

When I suggested to Fran the idea that she could change her perception of work, I met with a wall of resistance. She recognised that in her heart she wanted to change, but the learned cynicism made it a real challenge. When we explored her cynical outlook we discovered that it arose from fear that she would feel hurt and betrayed again. Accepting the feeling of fear enabled her to consider that she could have a different experience of work. I asked her to suspend judgement as to the likelihood of this happening and start by redefining her outlook on work. Fran created a new vision for work which read:

Work is a creative and enjoyable challenge from which I derive a sense of achievement and deserved recognition. I am valued and respected for my contribution, and it gives me an enjoyable and rewarding standard of living.

She then went on to make a six-point plan of what she wanted:

1. To work in an environment of support, praise, inspiration and success – for myself and others.
2　For work to be fulfilling.
3. To have rewarding relationships with people.
4. To have time to follow other pursuits.
5. For work to give me more balance in life.
6. For work to allow me the standard of living that I am accustomed to.

I asked Fran the key question: 'What would need to happen in order for you to create that work?' Her first response was, 'To change my opinion about work!' This turned out to be the turning point for her. By taking responsibility for her experience of work she was able to let go of the past pain and focus on landing her ideal job.

The leap that Fran made was one of possibility, vision and choice. This is available to each one of us, but it is down to our willingness and commitment to make the leap.

> **Exercise:** My new meaning of work is . . .
> What I want in my work is . . .

Emotional Confidence at Work

What is it for you? Stress, anxiety, anger, lethargy, boredom, guilt, frustration, fear? Whatever emotions you experience at work you probably tend to keep them to yourself. The fear of your colleagues or boss finding out how you really feel ensures that you have learned to give a good performance when you are not feeling at your best. When I have worked with teams to create a healthier emotional atmosphere, people agree with the principle – but find the application a challenging concept.

If you work in a culture that places little importance on emotional wellbeing, then the onus is on you to 'check in' and monitor how you are feeling. This is vital to ensure that there isn't a build-up of emotional residue, which impacts on the rest of your life. On numerous occasions I have heard that the major complaint in a relationship is that one person, or both, brings the emotional content of their work home with them. Obviously there will be an overlap, especially if your work holds great meaning and purpose for you, but if you are experiencing emotional difficulty it is supportive for yourself and the relationship to handle these feelings away from the relationship.

The work journal

A useful way to 'check in' and express your feelings is to keep a journal specifically for recording your emotions linked to work. Write down your feelings about any aspect of work: projects, people, deadlines, expectations, roles, responsibilities, regulations, money, time. Do not edit how you feel. This journal is for your eyes only so you have total freedom to say what you feel. By doing this over a period of time you help to clear any emotional backlog, as well as giving space to current issues that you are facing. By applying the four steps of emotional healing – awareness, acceptance, release and choice – you gain clarity and confidence about handling your emotions at work.

We all need to offload our feelings since it is inevitable that during the course of a working day, irritations, frustrations and pressures will arise. Even when you do work that you love, there are challenges to be faced as you liaise with customers, colleagues and suppliers. The emotional journal provides the space for you to complain, moan and gossip about people and events with the purpose of letting feelings go. It is difficult to be truly effective at work if you are carrying grudges and grievances from the past. If there is one person in particular that you are experiencing conflict with, it is a powerful process to write how you feel about them with the intention of overcoming the problems. Your *intention* is the key here: this ensures that you take responsibility for your part in the relationship and clarify any issues that you may be projecting on to this person.

A close friend of mine called Paul experienced feelings of anger that appeared out of proportion in one working relationship. His colleague was in a slightly senior position to him and each time Paul wanted to implement a new idea he found that this person would oppose the concept. The strength of his anger was such that it stopped him from being able to talk directly to his colleague about the situation. It got to the stage where he thought that he might have to look for another job because the very sight of this person would activate the anger. When Paul worked with the journal he realised that this colleague reminded him of his father, who always put down his ideas as insignificant. He saw that he had internalised the message that he was insignificant, and that he projected this thought on to his colleague. He understood that until he changed this belief and released the anger he would recreate this dynamic in another relationship. By going to the source of his feelings Paul was able to resolve the emotional pattern, which enabled him to discuss his ideas in a constructive manner.

The emotional journal gives you the opportunity to dig down under your immediate feelings and discover other layers of emotion. It is also a useful way to discover if you have certain emotions that you lean towards at times of stress or conflict in work. For some people it is common to feel anger, for others frustration or disillusionment. A useful way to distinguish an emotional pattern from the experience of daily feelings is to notice how you feel when you scan all aspects of work in your mind. If you feel relatively calm and peaceful then you are in denial. (No. I'm just kidding!) This shows that you are clear at the moment. If there is one emotion that recurs when you do this, by investing the time in writing about it you expand your awareness, which empowers you to identify the dynamic lying behind the feeling. This then enables you to make new choices, and break the recurring cycle.

It's good to talk

British Telecom got it right in its campaign to promote the idea that it's good to talk. The ideal way of creating emotional confidence at work is to be able to talk about how you feel. Working in a culture in which people are encouraged to air their feelings resolves conflict, aids creativity and lowers stress. It is important to clarify that I am not advocating that work become an opportunity for group therapy, simply that people have the right to say how they feel without fear of losing their job or reputation. This can seem a tall order in low-trust cultures, but having the courage to be emotionally honest creates a ripple effect within a working environment, building trust and respect.

I observed this with a client who complained that after working for one year in her current job she felt that she wasn't being given the level of responsibility she wanted and that she believed that her boss held a personal grudge against her. We set up an imaginary role-play where she expressed to her boss how she felt. She made the following statement in an attacking tone: 'You obviously don't respect me because you never give me the responsibility I deserve. You pass on work and opportunity to my colleagues and you always leave me out. I'm considering leaving because I don't know how much longer I can take it.' I asked her to imagine how her boss would receive that communication. She admitted that he would probably become angry, defensive and welcome her decision to leave.

We then looked at the option of taking responsibility for her feelings and asking for what she wanted. In another role-play she practised this by saying in an open tone, 'I would like to discuss with you my role in the company. During the course of this year I have enjoyed my work. I would be interested to know the direction we are moving in since I would welcome the opportunity to take on further responsibility. I believe that I need to be stretched and given fresh challenges in order to develop and stay motivated.' When I asked her how she thought her boss might respond to that statement she believed that he would respond positively since he appreciated proactive behaviour. Having rehearsed the communication she plucked up the courage to request a meeting. She started off by finding out her boss's opinion on the current state of affairs and then put her position forward. The outcome was a pay rise, increased responsibility and new challenges.

Developing emotional confidence through raising your awareness of your feelings, and learning how to express them constructively, enables you to let go of the pressures and demands of work and to maintain a sense of perspective. Asking yourself the question, 'Will this matter a year from now?' is a useful way to remember what is really important.

Heartfelt communication

A major belief associated with work is that you have to be compliant in your communication. Often the only perceived alternative is to rebel and either leave your place of work or gain the reputation of being a troubleshooter. There is another option, which has integrity, authenticity and is solution-orientated – heartfelt communication. This is when you communicate from a place of openness, co-operation and trust. Unfortunately, many people's experience of work has been damaged by their involvement in hierarchical structures which haven't allowed their individual voice to be heard. We are now living in an age when these structures and systems are undergoing vast changes and the responsibility now lies with each individual, giving us the opportunity to be resourceful and creative in our thinking, communication and performance.

If you fail to communicate authentically you leave yourself in a vulnerable position. Once you start communicating from either a compliant or a rebellious stance, a pattern is established that is difficult to break. It creates tension and disillusionment to go against your true nature. Consider the following idea from Abe Wagner, a management consultant: 'Say it straight or you'll show it crooked.' This implies that unless your communication and behaviour are congruent there will be a discrepancy between what you say and what you do.

The truly great world leaders are those who have led by example. There is a lovely story told about Gandhi. A mother implored him to tell her son to stop eating so much sugar, as his teeth were rotting. Gandhi replied, 'Bring him back in two weeks.' So the woman duly took her son away and returned two weeks later. This time Gandhi told the boy, 'You really should stop eating so much sugar, and you will preserve your teeth.' The mother thanked him, and then asked, 'But why couldn't you tell him that when we came two weeks ago?' Gandhi responded, 'Because two weeks ago I was still eating sugar!' This story embodies Gandhi's view that, 'We must be the change we want to see in the world.'

When you communicate from the heart you live according to your values and this brings you a great sense of peace and fulfilment. You will fail to experience true success as long as you communicate from a place of fear. If you perceive the world of work through the eyes of fear, it is your willingness to see it differently that will set you free. Each day decide that you are going to be more authentic than the day before, and notice what happens. The first day you might fear that you will not survive the 24 hours, but as time goes on and you stay committed to a path of heartfelt communication you will reap the benefits of living a life of integrity and true service.

Relationships at Work

> We are prone to judge success by the index of our salaries
> or the size of our automobiles rather than by the quality of
> our service and relationship to mankind. *Martin Luther
> King*

In our world of high technology and information where the PC, e-mail, web site, fax machine, answer machine and automated calling system dominate, it is easy to forget that behind all this high tech are human beings. I find it eerie to walk into an office environment and see row upon row of humans linked to machines with hardly any human contact on show. No wonder we are experiencing computer rage and desk rage, where people's frustrations get taken out on inanimate objects. We are social creatures who need to be integrated with each other. Relationships offer the potential for us to experience our greatest joy in work.

We have become our own worst enemies in the area of nurturing relationships in the work environment, allowing systems to take over our basic needs. In the caring field, for example, GPs have a 5–7-minute time slot in which to see a patient. During that time they are expected to diagnose and treat a condition which often requires a listening ear. The physician Patch Adams explains how, as a family doctor, he made house calls for twenty-eight years. He believes that the quality of the relationship he develops with a patient is fundamental to the healing process. In your working life you may not be dealing with people who are suffering illness, but the same principle applies: the quality of the relationships you develop are at the centre of your enjoyment and success. You do not succeed alone. The old saying, 'It's not what you know, it's who you know' is popular in the work arena. I would take that one step further and say that it's the quality of the relationship with who you know that makes the difference.

A dynamic to become aware of is that we project unresolved relationship issues from the past on to current relationships. It is a common scenario for a boss to represent a parent and a colleague to remind us of a sibling, friend or previous colleague. I counselled a client, Julian, who was struggling in his relationship with his boss. He felt undermined and lived in fear of incurring disapproval. When I asked him who his boss reminded him of, he immediately said his father. He had always felt afraid of his father and had tried to win his approval, but felt he could never live up to his expectations. By going to the root of the problem he could work on resolving his relationship with his father. Using the technique of completion letters Julian released his fear of his father and was able to focus on how he would like to feel in the relationship – equal, safe and supported. He was then able to carry this blueprint into his relationship with his boss. He was surprised to find that by shifting his perception of his boss he felt empowered and liberated from seeking his approval. He performed more effectively now he was working from his heart rather than from fear.

Think about who you work with or for, and see who they remind you of from the past. Does your boss represent a parental figure, and if so what aspect of your relationship with that parent? Do your colleagues remind you of siblings, friends or previous colleagues, and if so how would you describe those relationships?

Exercise: Think of the most successful people that you know personally and describe the quality of work relationships they create.

Having focused on developing the inner aspects of a working life, the following section focuses on enhancing the outer aspects in order to create fulfilling and rewarding work.

CREATIVITY AT WORK

Your work is to discover your work, and then with all your heart to give yourself to it. *Buddha*

Growing up as a musician I always had a fascination with

creativity and the creative process. I wondered how Bach could create music of such exquisite beauty and perfection, how Beethoven could write masterpieces while suffering from a hearing loss towards the end of his life, how Mozart could produce more memorable music in twenty-five years of life than one could possibly imagine. My other major passion when growing up was football, in particular Leeds United. In the 1970s they were an inspired team playing magical football that put them in the record books. It was a thrill to watch a team blend individual talent and flair and turn it into great success. The extraordinary element in all these feats was that they were people's work. It showed me that it was possible for creativity and work to go hand in hand.

It might not be everybody's purpose or desire to be a musician or sports person, but we can all discover the gift of creativity whatever our chosen field of work. There is a common mis-understanding that creativity is limited to artistic worlds. Yet I have certainly found that in running my own business there is the same opportunity to express creativity as when I was a violinist. Each day we bring into being thoughts, ideas, projects, hopes and relationships. Our intrinsic nature is to create and by recognising this we open ourselves to living an inspired life.

In order to recover our creativity we need to dispel the popular myth that only a minority of people are creative. Some of the main beliefs that block our creativity are:

- I cannot be creative because I haven't trained to be an artist.
- Creative people have special gifts, which I don't have.
- If I follow my creativity I won't be able to earn a living.
- To be successful creatively you have to sell your soul.
- It's egocentric to think that I'm creative.
- It's too late in my life; I'd have done it by now if I could

These types of belief become excuses that stop you from finding your creative potential. Write down some of the blocks that prevent you from discovering your creativity. Since all change starts with awareness, the process of becoming conscious of your limiting beliefs changes the way you see yourself. Accessing your creativity is directly linked to your self-image. If you tell yourself, 'It's arrogant or egocentric' whenever you yearn for a more creative life you will remain creatively blocked. If on the other hand you perceive yourself as a creative being you open yourself to your creativity.

Some new beliefs that support your creativity are:

◆ I am willing to experience my creative energy.
◆ My creativity is inherent in my being.
◆ My creativity supports myself and others.
◆ As I follow my creativity, opportunities will present themselves.
◆ I am willing to be of service through my creativity.

Asking 'If I saw myself as a creative person how would it affect my work?' encourages you to develop ideas that you can implement if you choose. I had a client, Noel, who sought to unleash his creativity. He worked for a firm of accountants, a profession which is not renowned for its creative outlets. When he asked himself the above question he couldn't come up with any answers. He felt stuck and limited by his job description. I encouraged him to shift his focus from the form of his work to the essence of his work, helping others. By doing this Noel was able to see how he could respond creatively to his clients' needs. He recognised that most of his clients felt powerless *vis-à-vis* their accounts, due to their lack of knowledge and skill with numbers. He decided that he would invest greater attention in helping his clients understand them. He developed simple but effective methods that enabled his clients to take greater control of their finances, for which they were truly grateful. He enjoyed receiving the positive feedback but more importantly he could now explore creative possibilities that had been hidden from him before.

Children are wonderful teachers of creativity. When my godson Zach comes to stay, he asks for all the old cardboard toilet roll holders, empty food cartons, string, scissors and glue so that he can get to work on creating his imaginary world. We adults still have that innate ability within us. It takes some prompting and encouragement to get the creative juices flowing again. The starting point is to see yourself as a creative being and then to have the courage to follow your ideas. Keep a notebook handy so you can jot down thoughts that come into your mind as you wait for a train, walk to a destination or do the shopping. It is essential to be kind to these ideas and not to judge them as worthless, useless or pie in the sky. Often as we start to tap into our creativity we have to face our doubts, our inner cynics, the voices that say, 'Who do think you are anyway? Anything of value or use has already been done, so why bother?' If we all followed that line of thought, we would never follow through on any ideas.

When I started writing this book I was racked with self-doubt and insecurity. I focused on the countless number of personal development books and told myself that it had all been said before, and what did I have to offer? I had to remind myself that we all have our own unique talents and experience and trust that my approach was valid and useful. The Nike mantra 'Just do it' is the absolute truth when it comes to developing our creativity. Our creative confidence grows as we exercise our creative muscle. Starting in small ways is the route forward. Wake up ten minutes earlier in the morning to take a short walk, read an inspiring book or listen to an inspirational tape on the way to work. Take some flowers into your work environment. Start a think-tank with colleagues to brainstorm creative ideas. Visit an art gallery once a month, listen to uplifting music, talk to people whom you consider creative and discover their secrets. Commitment to the development of your creativity is the key. As the German writer Goethe said:

Until one is committed, there is hesitancy, the chance to draw back, always ineffectiveness. Concerning all acts of initiative (and creation) there is one elementary truth, the ignorance of which kills countless ideas and splendid plans: that the moment one definitely commits oneself, then providence moves too. All sorts of things occur to help one that would never otherwise have occurred. A whole stream of events issues from the decision, raising in one's favour all manner of unforeseen incidents and meetings and material assistance, which no man could have dreamed would come his way. Whatever you can do, or dream you can, begin it now. Boldness has genius, power and magic in it.

Several years ago I had the idea of starting an educational project for teenagers to help them lead happy and successful lives. I felt passionately about the plight of young people, as the pressure to be hip, cool, trendy and successful in exams was greater than ever. The trouble was I didn't have any contact with teenagers and I didn't expect them to welcome the idea of attending a seminar in their spare time. I committed to the idea and made contact with Scott, the teenage son of a client. He agreed to get some friends together as a pilot scheme. Thankfully they enjoyed the experience, which strengthened my conviction. I discussed it with more and more people and it turned out that one of the mothers whose daughters attended the workshop was a journalist for a national paper. Several weeks later I was called up for a photo shoot and within days a full-page feature came out. The project PROteen was born. Television and radio interviews followed and I even received an invitation from Buckingham Palace, since there was some royal interest in the scheme. None of these events would have occurred if I hadn't been willing to commit in the first place. The greatest joy of it all was being able to support young people at testing times in their lives.

Our task in bringing creativity into our work is not to figure out all the details of how we are going to do it, but to make a commitment to live authentically and with passion. This is what we all yearn for in our working lives: to express our whole unique selves.

> **Exercise:** Take some time to be still, and ask yourself the question, 'If I were to put creativity, my creative ideas and my creative capacity centre stage in my life, what might that look like?' Note what thoughts and ideas come to you. Commit to following through on one idea, no matter how small.

Inspiration at work

> When you work only for yourself, or for your own personal
> gain, your mind will seldom rise above the limitations of an
> undeveloped personal life. But when you are inspired by
> some great purpose, some extraordinary project, all your
> thoughts break your bonds: your mind transcends limita-
> tions, your consciousness expands in every direction, and
> you find yourself in a new, great and wonderful world.
> Dormant forces, faculties and talents become alive, and
> you discover yourself to be a greater person by far than you
> ever dreamed yourself to be. *Patanjali*, Indian philosopher

The *Oxford English Dictionary* defines *inspiration* as the drawing in
of breath. Since breath gives rise to life you are literally drawing
in life when you are inspired. Another way of looking at
inspiration is that it means to be 'in-spirit'. When you are in the
zone of spirit you are connected with the essence of life. Spirit is
energy and all matter is made up of energy. When you are
inspired you experience greater energy and power because you
are more consciously linked to the level of energy that is available
to you. The more time that you spend in an inspired state, the
more your consciousness expands.

We all have a voice of inspiration. To make inspiration a
priority in our lives we must discover the aspects of life that
cultivate inspiration, and the aspects that take it away.

For example, notice which people uplift and motivate you and
which people leave you feeling drained and exhausted. Notice
which activities inspire you and which cause you irritation and
boredom. Become aware of the effects of the food you eat and
notice which foods cause you to feel heavy and weighed down
and which foods cause you to feel energised and nourished.
Notice the effects that environments have on you: which cause
you to feel relaxed and open, and which zap your energy, leaving
you exhausted and deadened. Notice the effects that the literature
you read has on you, the difference between words that uplift and
inspire you and those that disturb your peace of mind. In
particular notice which aspects of your work inspire you and

which frustrate you. Once you have discovered what nurtures your inspiration, commit to those things. You cannot control or manipulate inspiration but you can certainly choose and encourage it.

One of the most powerful questions you can ask yourself is the following: 'If I only did work that truly inspired me, what would I be doing?' See what comes into your mind. Don't edit your responses, just make a note of them. Doing this on a regular basis helps to build the emotional muscle that enables you to follow through your ideas. Applying this question puts you in touch with a vision of how to bring inspiration into your current work or how to create inspiring work for yourself. A client of mine found his job threatened when the company he worked for was taken over by a larger organisation. He wasn't sure whether he wanted to work in the new structure but was reluctant to cut his ties. Through asking this question he realised that what he really wanted to do was to form his own company. He managed to negotiate a favourable redundancy package and then set the stage for creating his own business.

Think of people you know who do work that inspires them. What can you learn from them and how can they help you? If you have trouble thinking of any, then seek out people who clearly do enjoy and love their work. We all need role models in our lives: people who inspire us and people from whom we can learn. The practice of mentoring and coaching is becoming increasingly popular in our working culture. It is immensely supportive to have someone who guides and encourages you and who helps you to stay focused on your inspiration when doubts and fears emerge.

Doubts and fears block our inspiration. Michelangelo was once asked, 'How do you create your beautiful sculptures?' He responded, 'I do not create beauty, God creates beauty. I merely chip away the surrounding marble so as to reveal the beauty. The beauty is already within. It is already perfectly in place.' This is true of your inspiration. It is already present within you; your job is to chip away the fears, doubts and judgements so as to reveal the inspiration within. By turning to spirit and asking for help to undo your blocks you are using the source of inspiration to guide you. The following meditation is designed to reconnect you with your inspiration:

Exercise: Sit quietly and focus your attention on your breathing. With each in-breath repeat the word 'inspiration' and with each out breath repeat 'letting go'. After several minutes say to yourself:

'I am willing to let go of any subconscious fears, doubts or judgements that may block my inspiration. If I have mistakenly believed that inspired work is only for a lucky few, I am willing to transform that belief. If I have mistakenly believed that I was not deserving and worthy of doing inspired work, I am willing to change my mind about myself.

'Where I have felt that my work is less than it could be, that I cannot find my passion or my creativity and that I have squashed the potential within me, I am willing to release those chains that have trapped me. I am willing to see work differently.

'I open myself to a vocation of freedom, creativity and inspiration. I commit to building a new context for work and wealth, in which all people serve and benefit. I dedicate my work to the good of all mankind.

'May I be guided each step of the way. May I discover and use my unique gifts and talents to enrich the lives of others.

'I open myself to being in the right place, at the right time and doing the right thing. I open my mind to possibilities I have not imagined, to forces of life I have blocked and to realms of joy I have not yet conceived.

'I free and release myself from anything that stands in the way between me and doing inspirational, meaningful and rewarding work.'

Creating the work you love

What lies behind us and lies before us are small matters

compared to what lies within us. And when we bring what is within out into the world, miracles happen. *Henry David Thoreau*, writer

You simply don't know what you are capable of until you start going for it. Whether you are seeking to create the work of your dreams or you want to transform your current work, following these seven steps ensures that you are on the right path.

Develop self-belief

A person is as he believes. *Anton Chekhov*

Believing in yourself gives you the confidence to create the work you love and to change your current work for the better. Self-belief can be achieved by constantly taking small steps in the direction you want to be heading. It is like developing your physical body: it would be a mistake to believe that one ultimate workout in the gym will give you the type of physique you want. To build your physical muscles requires repetition, repetition and repetition. This is equally true of building your self-belief. You have already taken one major step by reading this book and equipping yourself with the necessary information. Another step is to follow the exercises and ideas in the book rather than thinking, 'Good idea, I'll do it tomorrow.' Procrastination is one of the main blocks to developing self-belief. Putting off what could be done today delays the benefits of believing in yourself. A further step would be to create a positive affirmation for yourself to enhance your self-image. Since life reflects the way you see yourself, the higher you see yourself the better your life becomes.

Remember that 'life is on your side'
Do you tend to think that life is for you, or against you? Sometimes it can feel as if the world is out to get you, that everything that could possibly go wrong seems to happen. It is at such times that your faith in the inherent goodness of life is put to the test. Remember that the way you respond to these challenges will

determine the outcome. If you slip into a victim mentality, believing that life is against you, you will lose confidence and motivation. If you choose to connect with the intelligence behind life which guides all things, you will feel trusting, safe and protected. Life wants you to create what you love and to prosper. This is everybody's birthright. Just imagine the power that would be generated if everybody knew that life was on their side and that they were doing what they loved. By focusing on this image you tap into the spiritual potential that is available to each one of us.

Have vision

> Without this playing with fantasy no creative work has ever yet come to birth. The debt we owe to the play of the imagination is incalculable. *Carl Jung*

Continue to dream and dare. Play with your imagination and let ideas spring forth. Discover ways of encouraging your vision to develop. Some ideas include spending time in nature, meditation and silence, going to art galleries, listening to music, reading inspiring and visionary literature and seeking out visionary leaders and hearing their talks. Do not try to force your vision: this implies a sense of doubt, which is a reflection of fear. Your vision will flow from a peaceful heart, so cultivate an inner sanctuary and time to be with your heart and soul. As Picasso said: 'Nothing can be achieved without solitude.' One of the most powerful things I have ever done was to spend 48 hours in silence, solitude and seclusion. I booked myself into a single room in a monastery without a watch, any reading or writing material, and faced my demons. During the first 12 hours I watched every fearful thought pass through my mind. Following a period of sleep I experienced a tremendous feeling of peace and calm as if I had been cleansed. For the rest of the time I enjoyed connecting with uplifting and inspiring thoughts. You do not have to go to that extreme, but making sure you have regular time alone in silence will help you to develop your vision.

Take action

> The universe rewards actions. *Robert Redfern*, business entrepreneur

You will clarify your vision by taking action on the ideas you already have. Be aware that the ego can sabotage your success by preventing you from following through on your ideas. Some of the main ways that sabotage shows up are:

- telling yourself that your ideas are no good, or that they have all been done before;
- not contacting people or returning phone calls of people who are interested in you or your work;
- keeping yourself too busy with other things and not giving yourself time to focus on what is important to you.

One useful technique is to write down three 'must do' items at the beginning of each day. These 'must do' items are things of real value to you and may be linked to the work you are currently doing or to developing your vision. For example, meditate, call a friend for lunch, finish a project, read an article, make important phone calls. Then commit to doing what is on your list before anything else. By doing this you develop the habit of doing what is valuable to you first in your day, until eventually everything in your life has great value for you.

Practise non-attachment
We must learn to let go of our emotional attachment to our vision and actions in order for them to materialise. When we become attached we function from a place of fear. When we let go, we affirm our wholeness. A crucial point here is not to confuse non-attachment with a lack of interest. We feign non-attachment when we act uninterested, as we are protecting ourselves from possible loss, hurt, rejection or disappointment. True non-attachment is when we genuinely surrender to the outcome of events without trying to manipulate or control them. This can feel like a big risk but opens the door to a life of freedom and joy. I have discovered

that when I practise non-attachment in the work environment it enables me to truly serve my clients. This is because my attention is on how can I help them, rather than on wondering what's in it for me. It also ensures that I am fully present in the here and now rather than projecting into the future. This improves the quality of my work and level of fulfilment.

Develop your compassion

Creating the work you love is a constant and never-ending journey. You will encounter obstacles and challenges along the route that test your resilience, trust and patience. The way forward is to develop your compassion for yourself and others so that you are anchored in love, understanding and empathy. These qualities act as a compass to guide you at times of stress and anxiety and to lead you towards true service, which is the essence of creating fulfilling work. The development of compassion involves the practice of acceptance. When you genuinely accept yourself and others you open your heart and expand your motives to what and who truly matters in life and work. You move beyond striving for personal achievement in work and commit to enhancing the welfare of others. Compassion increases your sense of gratitude by taking your attention off all the little things that can cause you to worry and putting it on the great gifts that life offers you.

Celebrating your successes as you go

Since true success is a way of travelling, not an ultimate destination, it is essential to take the time to celebrate the small successes along the way. Notice the temptation to have an ultimate goal that you can never quite reach, which keeps fulfilment and enjoyment on tomorrow's agenda rather than today's. Commit to focusing on what is good and working now, rather than being caught in the ego's conditions of more, better, when, if and maybe. This includes celebrating apparent failure because from each mistake comes learning and growth. Finding and creating the work you love may well bring you financial and material rewards in the future, but by far the greatest reward is to value and appreciate your life now. The truth is, you do not know how long you are going to live. Making the most of today ensures that you commit to what's truly important in your life – your family, your friends, your health and your happiness – as well as getting the job done!

In Conclusion

Let us live so well even the undertaker will be sorry to see us go! *Mark Twain*

When people come to the end of their life and look back, they tend not to wish that they had spent an extra day in the office, had accumulated a little more money in the bank account or had achieved their ideal body weight. Their attention is placed on the truly important things in life – were they a loving partner, a good parent, a compassionate citizen?

There are three key questions to reflect upon that go to the very centre of maintaining a balanced path in life:

◆ Did I love well?
◆ Did I live fully?
◆ Did I learn to let go?

When you love well you extend yourself to others, you serve, you contribute and you learn that your loving presence does make a difference. You touch the lives of others by offering compassion, empathy and understanding. You come to recognise that love is at the heart of your happiness and success. *A Course in Miracles* tells us: 'Teach only love, for that is what you are.' By loving you connect to your purpose in life. You release the judgement, fear and guilt that hold you back from living fully and you experience the joy, peace and abundance that come from being who you truly are.

When you live fully you engage in the creative process of life that enables you to fulfil your potential. This is not measured by how much money you make, or promotions you achieve or the like. Rather it is how true you are to yourself: not in a selfish sense, but whether you live your life on purpose, and take the necessary risks to follow your heart. There is a lot of truth in the saying, 'Life is not a dress rehearsal.' Yet sometimes it can seem as if you are still auditioning for a part, let alone reaching the dress rehearsal! You only get one opportunity to live in this body, at this moment in time. It is your responsibility to seize the gift of each day and to live it as if it were your last, because it might be! You can forget how precious each moment is. You can live life so far ahead of each day, with imaginary fears dominating your mind, that you become removed from the possibilities that are here, now, today.

I once worked with a young woman who was dying of cancer. She had a twin sister who was pregnant at the same time that she was suffering the later stages of her illness. It was a poignant time for all involved and I shall always remember the dying woman saying that her greatest sadness lay in the fact that she felt that she had not lived fully. She had considered herself less attractive and capable than her sister, and as a result had never committed fully to a relationship, to work and to living, believing that what she had to offer was insignificant. It was only on her deathbed that she was able to forgive and let go of the grievances and troubles that had plagued her life. This enabled her to make peace with herself and leave this world with a sense of wholeness and completion.

Letting go helps you to stay present in the midst of change and challenges. Since change is inevitable, the more deeply you can learn to let go, the more you can respond to it with trust and confidence. Letting go returns you to love because once you drop the baggage that you carry, only love remains. The story of the discovery of the Golden Buddha in Bangkok illustrates this. Back in 1957 a group of monks had to relocate a clay Buddha from their temple to a new site. During the move, the clay covering the Buddha began to crack and at first they feared that they might have damaged the great idol. What they discovered was that underneath the clay casing was a solid gold Buddha. It transpired that at a time of war several hundred years before, monks had covered the Buddha with clay to protect it from being stolen. Your fears, doubts and judgements make up your own coverings of clay. When you allow your hard casing to soften you discover the golden Buddha within.

LIFE IS NOT AN EMERGENCY

An important aspect of letting go is to slow down. We often spend our lives in the fast lane, yet we still don't seem to be going fast enough. One of the greatest lessons for experiencing true success is to know when enough is enough. Otherwise you never have a finishing line, and frustration and disappointment ensue. It can feel as if you are going to miss out on the goodies if you take your foot off the accelerator. This is a self-induced fear that prevents you from being true to yourself. When you start living life with the belief that you have enough time to do everything you want to do, you relax, enjoy what you're currently doing and become more effective.

To end the emergency you need to unlearn the idea that more is better, faster is smarter and urgency is importance. As long as you continue to believe that more is better, you will never be fulfilled because as soon as you have accomplished something, you go rushing on to the next thing – immediately. I have noticed this trait in myself while on holiday. One of my favourite activities is walking. It puts me in the present moment and gives me peace of mind. The trouble is that I prevent myself from enjoying this peace by thinking of the next walk, telling myself that the more walks I do, the better the holiday I'll have! Notice the areas in your life where you believe more is better. Letting go of this idea doesn't mean that you stop going for more in your life, it just means that you start appreciating what you already have and that your happiness is not dependent on getting, owning or having more.

We live in a world where the mentality of speed dominates. We get frustrated with our computers for taking the time of a breath to save valuable information, we get irritated waiting for the photocopier to warm up, we fume while sitting in traffic jams and we eat fast food on the run. Although speed is convenient, a life on the run is full of stress, anxiety and indigestion. I love the motto, 'Slowly is holy', which reminds me to slow down, stop and smell the roses and make the most of today.

To live your life in a rush causes you to forget what is truly important. Suddenly everything seems to have an 'urgent' sign hanging over it and your life becomes one great big crisis to manage. Although you can gain a sense of achievement from handling a crisis, jumping from one crisis to the next eventually leads to burnout. Remembering what really matters and putting that first counteracts this habit of urgency. Make sure that you have your five most important ideals written down and carry them with you wherever you go. We need constant reminders to stay focused on what we value. In my wallet I have a photograph of Veronica alongside a card with the words 'love, people, being, enjoyment and success' written on it.

Are you enjoying the journey?

We have noted that success is a journey, not a destination. One of the key criteria along the way is enjoyment. When you enjoy life, you rise to its challenge rather than trying to hide from it. To ensure your enjoyment there is one key question to ask yourself:

> How do I know at the end of a day if I have enjoyed it or not?

Establishing a clear criterion for enjoyment on a daily basis ensures that you stop waiting for the weekend, the two-week holiday, the promotion, the pay rise or the finished project, and encourages you to enjoy the whole of your life, now. The following are my criteria for enjoyment on a daily basis:

- seeing the day as a new opportunity
- being grateful for the gift of the day
- being kind to myself
- touching the life of at least one person
- having the attitude of service within my work
- practising compassion
- putting love first

- committing to self-acceptance
- saying a genuine 'thank you' to someone
- using my creativity
- remembering that I am what I seek
- not taking myself too seriously
- taking time for silence
- working to the best of my ability
- learning something new
- eating something delicious
- playing some sport
- following my conscience
- having some fun.

This is very different from my old criteria for an enjoyable day, which included:

- achieving everything on my 'to do' list
- creating several new work opportunities
- pushing myself as hard as I can
- having a punishing workout in the gym

As you can see, I have learned to become more flexible. My fear of changing my criteria was that I would stop achieving and moving forward. What I have discovered is that the quality of my life has improved, I achieve more now than I ever used to and I enjoy the process. Discovering and honouring your criteria for enjoyment ensures lasting happiness and success.

WHAT WOULD YOU LIKE TO BE REMEMBERED FOR?

One of the most powerful ways to define what is important to you is to reflect on what you would like to be remembered for. I doubt very much that you would like to be remembered for being a highly stressed achiever, who put work and money before family, friends and health, although many of us do that without thinking of the long-term consequences. We go charging through life and it often takes a serious crisis to wake us up to our true priorities. When I have discussed this idea with people, the overwhelming majority say that they would like to be remembered for the type of person they were, rather than for their accomplishments. This is not to say that accomplishing things is invalid, far from it. But the means of achieving them and the type of person you become in the process is as important, if not more so, than the end result.

The truth is that you come into the world with nothing and you leave the world with nothing, but you do leave a legacy to the world that you create while you are here. For example, committing to becoming a more loving, giving and compassionate person means that you will be remembered for aspiring to principles that contribute to the wellbeing of everyone. This may seem a lofty ideal, but it can translate into practical everyday communications and actions that bring you true success.

A powerful method of getting in touch with how you would like to be remembered is to write your own obituary. Make sure that you include your personal and professional life, focusing on your characteristics, achievements, contributions, values and relationships. Although you might find this idea quite morbid it provides you with a blueprint for living your life on purpose.

Before enlightenment chop wood carry water, after enlightenment chop wood carry water. Zen proverb

There was a lady who looked after her elderly mother at home and didn't have a life of her own. She came to see me because she was unable to go to work or to have a normal social life. We looked at the various options but in the end the turning point came about not from changing the circumstances of her life, but through changing the way that she saw her life. By choosing to see her life as a gift, she was able to enjoy and make the most of each new day. This reinforced for me the principle that although you cannot always change your external reality – you might not even want to – what you can do is to transform your perception of reality.

True success is a continuing upward spiral, shifting your perception from fear to love, from scarcity to abundance and from conflict to peace. As you stop searching for success outside yourself and turn your attention inwards to the centre of your being, you live from your heart and allow yourself to appreciate and enjoy the miracle of life.

Suggested Reading

Anatomy of an Illness as Perceived by the Patient.
Norman Cousins (Bantam Books, 1981)
A powerful story affirming my belief that laughter is the best medicine.

Ancient Wisdom, Modern World.
Dalai Lama (Little, Brown and Company, 1999)
Inspiring teachings from a man who is a living example of compassion and wisdom.

The Artist's Way.
Julia Cameron (Pan Books, 1994)
A great workbook for discovering and recovering your creative self.

Britain on the Couch.
Oliver James (Arrow Books, 1998)
An in-depth study explaining why we're unhappier than we were in the 1950s – despite being richer.

Calm at Work.
Paul Wilson (Penguin Books, 1997)
I keep this handy just in case . . .

Chicken Soup for the Soul.
Jack Canfield, Mark Victor Hansen, Maida Rogerson, Martin Rutte and Ian Clauss (Vermilion, 1999)
A useful tonic when you need to lift your spirits.

A Course in Miracles.
(Penguin/Arkana, 1975)
I use this when I lie down and need a headrest! The definitive guide to spiritual psychology. Don't be put off by the Christian terminology. Consists of a complex text, 365 lessons and includes a manual for teachers. Helpful to study in a group.

Don't Sweat the Small Stuff . . .
Richard Carlson, Ph.D. (Hodder & Stoughton, 1997)
A great reminder of what's really important in life.

Emotional Intelligence.
Daniel Goleman (Bloomsbury, 1996)
A pioneering study of emotions.

Essays on Creating Sacred Relationships.
Sondra Ray (Celestial Arts, 1996)
The next step to a new paradigm.

Feel the Fear and Do It Anyway.
Susan Jeffers, Ph.D. (Rider, 1991)
The title alone reminds me to take the steps to freedom.

Happiness NOW!
Robert Holden (Hodder & Stoughton, 1998)
The essence of Robert's pioneering work in happiness. An essential read.

If It Hurts It Isn't Love.
Chuck Spezzano. (Hodder & Stoughton, 1998)
A brilliant book for relationship success.

Love, Medicine and Miracles.
Bernie Siegel, MD (Rider, 1986)
A wonderful book demonstrating the power of love.

Loving Relationships I.
Sondra Ray
This book changed my relationships for ever.

Man's Search for Meaning.
Viktor Frankl (Washington Square Press, 1984)
A powerful account of Frankl's survival of the Nazi death camps.
Gives a new perspective on life.

Manifest Your Destiny.
Wayne Dyer (HarperCollins, 1997)
Spiritual principles for getting what you want in life.

Men Are From Mars, Women Are From Venus.
John Gray, Ph.D. (HarperCollins, 1992)
A valuable guide to understanding the communication styles of
men and women.

Molecules of Emotion.
Candace Pert, Ph.D. (Simon & Schuster, 1997)
A brilliant account of why you feel the way you feel.

Open Heart Therapy.
Bob Mandel (Celestial Arts, 1984)
Inspiring insights into personal transformation.

A Path with Heart.
Jack Kornfield (Rider, 1994)
A beautiful book for learning about the heart of Buddhism.

A Return to Love.
Marianne Williamson (Thorsons, 1992)
An inspirational book based on the principles of *A Course in
Miracles.*

The Road Less Travelled.
Scott Peck, MD (Rider, 1978)
This book had a profound impact, steering me in the direction of
developing a loving and accepting approach to life.

The Seven Habits of Highly Effective People.
Stephen Covey (Simon & Schuster, 1989)
A superb model for enjoying a successful life.

The Seven Spiritual Laws of Success.
Deepak Chopra (New World Library, 1994)
Takes you on a journey to make your dreams come true.

The Work We Were Born To Do.
Nick Williams (Element, 1999)
A passionate book motivating you to find the work you love and
love the work you do.

Further Information

For further information on the work of Ben Renshaw and for details on public workshops, life coaching and corporate training contact:

Ben Renshaw
Clifton Gate
Clifton Avenue
London W12 9DR
Tel: 0208 762 0176
Fax: 0208 762 0176
E-mail: info@benrenshaw.com
Web site: www.happiness.co.uk

For further information on The Happiness Project and for details of public workshops, books and tapes, the 'Eight Week Happiness Programme', the 'Teaching Happiness' professional certificate training, or the 'Deep and Meaningful' corporate training programme, contact:

The Happiness Project
Elms Court
Chapel Way
Oxford OX2 9LP
Tel: 01865 244414
Fax: 01865 248825
E-mail: hello@happiness.co.uk
Web site: www.happiness.co.uk

Also available from Vermilion:

Together But Something Missing

How to Create and Sustain Successful Relationships

Ben Renshaw

Do you find relationships are like a rollercoaster? Let Ben Renshaw navigate you through their highs and lows. His insight, wit and practical tools will help you transform your experiences into a rich source of fulfilment and pleasure.

Full of new ideas, taking a wide-ranging approach, this inspiring and resourceful book shows you how to:

- know what you want
- break commitment phobia
- attract trust and intimacy
- improve communication
- let go of old heartbreak
- rise to the challenge of change
- open to love

Together But Something Missing is essential for anyone – whether single, married or with a partner – who wants to finally create relationship success.

The Secrets

100 Ways to Have a Great Relationship

Ben Renshaw

Are you looking for a fulfilling relationship? If so, *The Secrets* is required reading whether you are single or attached. Here is a book that reveals the *real* answers to the relationship rollercoaster. Have you found who you want to take on the ride, or are you still looking? Are you prepared to go the distance when the going gets tough, or are you going to jump off too early? Read this book and discover:

- The secret of finding the 'right' partner
- The secret of communicating successfully
- The secret of getting along
- The secret of having what you want
- The secret of making love last

Witty, honest and essential – *The Secrets* is your passport to a whole new relationship experience.

Feel the Fear and Do It Anyway

How to Turn Your Fear and Indecision into Confidence and Action

Susan Jeffers

- Public speaking
- Asserting yourself
- Making decisions
- Intimacy
- Changing jobs
- Being alone
- Ageing
- Driving
- Losing a loved one
- Ending a relationship

Everyone has such fears throughout their lives. But whatever *your* anxieties, this worldwide bestseller will give you the insight and tools to vastly improve your ability to handle any given situation. You will learn to live your life the way you want – so you can move from a place of pain, paralysis and depression to one of power, energy and enthusiasm.

This inspiring modern classic has helped thousands turn their anger into love – and their indecision into action – with Susan Jeffers' simple but profound advice to 'Feel the fear and do it anyway'.

Feel the Fear Planner

90 Days to a Fuller Life

Susan Jeffers

Those who have read the incredible worldwide bestsellers, *Feel the Fear and Do It Anyway*, and *Feel the Fear . . . and Beyond* will recognise Susan Jeffers' brilliant idea of the 'Power Planner'. This is a step-by-step guide for incorporating all her strategies for developing a fuller, richer life in one, easy-to-use, simple chart. Each day, for three months, you write down things to be grateful for – and also give yourself tasks to fulfil that you find particularly difficult. These may be in the fields of relationships, friends, family, work, time off or spirituality.

By risking small steps at a time, supporting and encouraging yourself, you can certainly learn to enjoy your life in a more conscious, loving, giving and powerful way. And this book will help you to do so.

Just Do It *Now*

How to become the person you most want to be

Lynda Field

This uplifting and inspiring book is a step-by-step guide to the simple principles which lie behind the truth that we create our own reality. But more than that, it also shows you how to overcome a natural fear of change so you can make your vision of who you are match your vision of who you want to be. In this way you can learn how to harness every aspect of yourself (mind, body, spirit and emotions) to the task of bringing motivation and enthusiasm into all areas of your life.

Bestselling author Lynda Field offers original exercises, practical tips and techniques which she has specially designed for your unique and specific needs. 'You are a powerhouse of amazing energy,' she says. 'You can decide to make the most of your life: Just Do It *Now*.'

If you would like to order any of the following or to receive our catalogue please fill in the form below:

Together But Something Missing by Ben Renshaw   £8.99
The Secrets by Ben Renshaw   £4.99
Feel the Fear and Do It Anyway by Susan Jeffers   £6.99
Feel the Fear Power Planner by Susan Jeffers   £6.99
Just Do It *Now* by Lynda Field   £6.99

ALL VERMILION BOOKS ARE AVAILABLE THROUGH MAIL ORDER OR FROM YOUR LOCAL BOOKSHOP.

PAYMENT MAY BE MADE USING ACCESS, VISA, MASTER-CARD, DINERS CLUB, SWITCH AND AMEX, OR CHEQUE, EUROCHEQUE AND POSTAL ORDER (STERLING ONLY).

EXPIRY DATE .... SWITCH ISSUE NO.

SIGNATURE...

PLEASE ALLOW £2.50 FOR POST AND PACKING FOR THE FIRST BOOK AND £1.00 PER BOOK THEREAFTER.

ORDER TOTAL: £.................................... (INCLUDING P&P)

ALL ORDERS TO:
VERMILION BOOKS, BOOKS BY POST, TBS LIMITED, THE BOOK SERVICE, COLCHESTER ROAD, FRATING GREEN, COLCHESTER, ESSEX, CO7 7DW, UK.
TELEPHONE: (01206) 256 000
FAX: (01206) 255 914

NAME ....
ADDRESS ....
....

Please allow 28 days for delivery. Please tick box if you do not wish to receive any additional information. ☐

Prices and availability subject to change without notice.